# PREFABULOUS
## FOR
## EVERYONE

SHERI KOONES

Gibbs Smith
TO ENRICH & INSPIRE HUMANKIND

For Bryan, Kimberly, Abigail, and Amelia Warman with much love.

First Edition
27 26 25 24 23      5 4 3 2 1

Text © 2023 Sheri Koones

Front cover photo: © 2023 Martin Knowles
Back cover photos:
    Top left © 2023 Steve Simonsen
    Top right courtesy Yankee Barn Homes
    Middle left © 2023 Reed Fish
    Middle center © 2023 Luis Ayala/Ayala Vargas Architectural
    Middle right © 2023  Adam Powers
    Bottom left © 2023 Chaunte Vaughn
    Author photo © 2023 Annie Watson
Additional photographic credits are found on the opening page
of each chapter.

Published by
Gibbs Smith
P.O. Box 667
Layton, Utah 84041
1.800.835.4993 orders
www.gibbs-smith.com

Designed by Ryan Thomann and Virginia Snow

Printed and bound in China

Gibbs Smith books are printed on paper produced from
sustainable PEFC-certified forest/controlled wood source.
Learn more at www.pefc.org.

ISBN: 978-1-4236-6359-1
Library of Congress Control Number: 2022941929

# CONTENTS

# INTRODUCTION

It has been my pleasure over the years to closely watch the evolution of housing, which has vastly changed with time. These changes have occurred with the development of more energy efficient products, increased interest in environmental issues, the enactment of more stringent building codes, and the availability of equipment that now allows for healthier, more comfortable and energy efficient homes.

A big issue in North America is the tremendous shortage in housing. The number of households formed in the US has far exceeded the number of single-family houses being built. This shortage has led to substantially higher prices for the small number of houses now available for would-be homebuyers. The COVID-19 pandemic also reduced the number of houses being built and caused many supply chain disruptions. Local codes have limited the construction of smaller size houses in some areas, forcing builders to continue building larger, more expensive houses rather than creating several housing units on the same lot where a single house once stood. The **Raleigh Simple House** demonstrates an example of adding density to a community by building multiple houses on a lot that originally had only one home.

**Below:** The Raleigh Simple House.

4

## THE MARKET FOR SMALL HOUSES IS INCREASING

Along with the general shortage of housing, there is a tremendous need for more efficient small houses, as well as more affordable houses. All age groups are looking for more energy efficient, sustainable housing. People recently entering the job market and starting families are looking for small houses. They usually cannot afford large homes, nor do their lifestyles require it. Many prefer to live in a more minimalist manner. Rather than owning toys such as boats, jetskis, trailers, or even cars, they choose to rent when the need arises. These environmentally conscious generations have taken ecology classes and filled their water bottles at stations in their schools. This group is also more interested in experiences—traveling and sporting activities—rather than doing maintenance on a house and yard. They would ideally like to find affordable, energy efficient, low maintenance, small houses.

Older generations also create another major market for small houses. They are often downsizing from larger houses where they brought up their children, or they are choosing to live a different lifestyle in a different place—urban over rural or vice versa, or in a different area of the country altogether. Some might be more interested in travel and cultural activities than maintaining a large home and doing yardwork. And many must have a more efficient house to save on energy costs.

## THE GROWTH OF ACCESSORY DWELLING UNITS (ADUS)

Accessory dwelling units (ADUs) have created an excellent source of additional housing in some areas of North America where there are vast shortages. They were first seen in British Columbia, Canada, as laneway houses, which were built in

**Above:** Vineyard Vista.

the back lanes, replacing garages. Many municipalities in the United States have adapted ordinances to allow ADUs in their areas adding density without, in some cases, the need for large multihousing units, which often change the nature of the area. ADUs provide housing for young adults who can't afford to purchase elsewhere, older adults who want to live near family, and seasonal workers and other renters. Several beautiful ADUs and guest houses are demonstrated here, including the **Harrison Lane House** and the **Maris ADU.**.

**Below:** Harrison Lane House.

**Above:** Ashford WeeHouse.

## ENERGY EFFICIENCY AS A GROWING NEED

Building energy efficient homes using less fossil fuel has never been more important than it is today. This is not only because of the cost of energy, but because of what we realize the burning of fossil fuel does to the environment. The architects, builders, and manufacturers who have contributed to the construction of the houses in this book have gone to great lengths to find ways to include green and energy features to make these houses eco-friendly and less dependent on fossil fuel. Two of the houses in the book are Passive House certified, which requires limited fuel use.

## HOUSING REQUIRED AFTER NATURAL DISASTERS

Thousands of houses have also been decimated by raging fires and hurricanes. There is a tremendous need for ingenuity in developing new and plentiful housing to replace those dwellings that have been destroyed and building them safer against future disasters. Several houses are featured in this book that were rebuilt after being destroyed by either fire, such as the **Ashford WeeHouse** and **Malibu House,** or by hurricane, such as the **Tropical Panorama House.**

**Below:** Olive Passive House.

**Below:** Hive House.

## PREFAB CONSTRUCTION AS A SOLUTION

There has also been a severe labor shortage for single-family home construction that began before the COVID-19 pandemic but was then intensified by it. Some workers have become reluctant to work on construction sites, sometimes having to deal with harsh weather conditions. An excellent solution for this issue is construction utilizing prefab methods. Workers can continue to work full-time through all types of weather in controlled conditions rather than at the periodic jobs they get at on-site projects. There are also many other advantages to prefab construction, such as:

- Faster construction times
- Cost savings
- Eco-friendly benefits
- No wasted time with weather conditions limiting work
- Less annoyance to neighboring homes
- Fewer dumpsters as prefab doesn't create as many cutoffs and refuse
- Construction loans converted more quickly to mortgages because it is faster to build
- Less cost for change orders that are so common with site-built homes
- Full-time professionals building the house
- Close supervision of construction
- Quality control

In the past there have been misconceptions about prefab construction; some people still think of prefab construction as tacky and plain. However, the reality is, prefab houses are mostly indistinguishable from site-built ones. Almost any house that can be built on-site can be built at least partially in a factory. I believe the houses in this book demonstrate the variety and beauty of houses that can be prefabricated.

This book includes a variety of types of prefab methods including modular, panelization, structural insulated panels (SIPs), prefab metal framing, insulated concrete forms (ICFs), post and beam framing, and kit housing.

Prefab construction is becoming a larger part of the home market in general, with the current labor shortage and the desire by many to have their home built more quickly. This is particularly true of those who have lost their homes to natural disasters. More and more people are beginning to recognize the efficiency and other advantages of prefab and are opting to build their homes in that way.

**Below:** Thimbleberry House.

## MAKING SMALL HOUSES FEEL BIGGER THAN THEY ARE

After having downsized with my husband several years ago, I discovered firsthand the pleasures of living smaller. There is less responsibility, lower energy costs, less maintenance, and a coziness of being closer to family members. Those people I have interviewed who have downsized tell me that moving into a smaller house is liberating.

Small houses are optimal for homeowners when they are designed to feel larger than they are. This is accomplished through design features such as:

- Good lighting, both natural and electric
- Multipurpose spaces
- Excellent storage
- Open floor plans
- Natural transitions to outdoor space
- Good ventilation, both naturally and mechanically
- Creative furnishings
- High ceilings
- Light colors

Each of the houses shown here includes many of these characteristics, making them all look and feel more spacious than their actual footprint indicates.

## HOUSES FOR EVERYONE

Optimally in the future there will be increased housing for everyone—those with good-sized budgets and those with smaller ones. With the current shortage of houses in North America, there is a tremendous need for both types of housing. In this book you will find houses that demonstrate both ends of the spectrum. There are luxury homes and some more affordable ones. Some of these more affordable homes are being produced by several new companies, such as **Boxabl** and **Liv-Connected**, that work to build factory-made homes that meet high standards for energy and comfort.

I hope you will be inspired by the variety of houses in this book, and the creativity used to produce them. I aspire to help you see the many great options that are now available. Happy Housing!

**Above:** Conexus House.

# ACKNOWLEDGMENTS

As always, I am indebted to the homeowners, architects, builders, manufacturers, and other specialists who share their time, expertise, and experiences with me. A vital and essential part of this book are the photos, and I thank all the photographers who graciously contributed their beautiful work to this book.

I would not even consider writing these books without the skillful and meticulous work by my friend and skillful artist Chuck Lockhart, who has been with me through most of my books and is a delight to work with.

A major thanks to the team at Gibbs Smith—Madge Baird, Marci Monson, Lizzi Middleman, Kim Eddy, Virginia Snow, and Leslie Stitt—all wonderfully enthusiastic and incredibly professional.

Thank you to my friend Peter Chapman, who has been a great consultant on many of my books.

And, finally, thank you to my husband, Rob, who looks at more photos that he would probably like and endures a stressed-out wife now and again. And to my daughter, Alex; son, Jesse; and bonus-child, Mella, who forever cheer me on.

# THE MAYNARD HOUSE

## PANELIZED

**PHOTOGRAPHER**
Lindsay Raymondjack

**GENERAL CONTRACTOR**
New School Builders
(https:newschoolbuilders.com)

**PREFABRICATOR/DESIGNER**
Unity Homes (https:unityhomes.com)

**SIZE**
1,836 square feet

**LOCATION**
Waterbury, Vermont

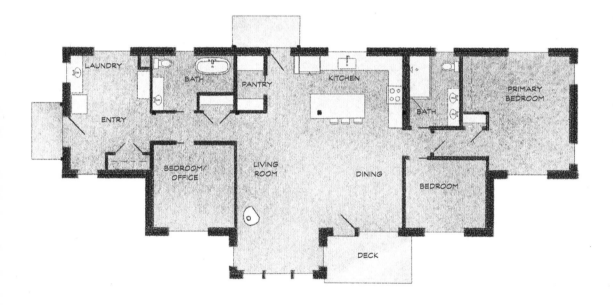

**M**any years ago, when they had difficulty finding locally grown garlic, Cindy and Bob Maynard bought property and started farming six acres of land with a variety of different types of garlic. They built a barn on the land to store their garlic and equipment and a large house at the other end of the 90-acre lot. When they found the two-mile travel back and forth to their garlic business was becoming excessive, they decided to build a house next to the barn and move closer to their business.

**Above:** The house was built close to the barn, which is used for storage and equipment for the couple's Green Mountain Garlic business.

## GREEN FEATURES

- Recycled metal roof and insulation
- Locally sourced products
- No gas used in the house
- Induction stove

## ENERGY FEATURES

- Triple-glazed windows
- Photovoltaic panels
- Air source heat pump
- Heat recovery ventilator (HRV)
- Heat pump water heater
- High efficiency insulation
- Highly insulated foundation

## AIRTIGHTNESS

- 0.65 ACH50 (just short of Passive House standards)

This came after their three children had moved out and their 6,000 square-foot home was beginning to feel excessively large. There were many rooms in the house that were not being used any longer. Their dream was to build a new house that was more energy efficient, easier to maintain, and closer to their business, so they sold their original too-big home.

**Above:** The house has an open concept design with cleverly placed post and beams to provide a subtle separation between the kitchen and the living/dining areas.

**Top:** The flooring in this farm-style kitchen is engineered white oak. The stove is an electric induction stove, which avoids the use of gas. A door in the kitchen area leads out to the barbecue area for easy access. A large walk-in pantry is used for storing the preserved vegetables they grow on the farm.

**Bottom:** The spacious dining area has a door leading out to the front porch, expanding the living and dining area.

## SELECTING A COMPANY TO BUILD THEIR HOME

The couple were attracted to Unity Homes because they were looking for companies that were building very energy efficient homes, designed with clean lines and had a modern aesthetic. Since they wanted the footprint to be small, it was important that there was an efficient use of space.

Cindy thought Unity's contemporary designed "Zum" home would also be an interesting contrast to the classic red barn already on the property. Since their large home sold within days of going on the market, it was important that their new house be built quickly. They knew that Unity's off-site fabrication would speed up construction time and provide greater cost predictability, compared with site-built houses. Cindy says, "The panelization system worked well for us, making the whole process much quicker than conventional construction. Having most of it built in the factory ensured us of better quality than having it built outdoors in harsh Vermont weather." She adds that Unity delivered what they promised and stood behind their work. It took just five months for the house to be completed once the design was approved.

**Right:** A small niche off the mud room is a perfect place for reading or just enjoying the beautiful scenery.

**Below:** The primary bedroom at the far end of the house is away from the common areas for extra privacy and quiet. The room is awash with abundant light from several tilt-and-turn windows, which can be open even when it's raining.

**Above, top:** Large overhangs protect the house from harsh Vermont winters and limit the hot summer rays.

**Above, bottom:** The barbecue area is at the rear of the house.

## BUILDING A NET ZERO HOME

One of the couple's priorities was to build their house as environmentally friendly and efficient as possible. The panels for this house are built thicker than usual, with dense-packed cellulose insulation for the walls and roof. The tilt-turn triple-glazed windows also provide a high degree of insulation. The heat recovery ventilation (HRV) system helps keep the air in the house fresh and healthy while windows are kept closed in the colder weather.

A blower door test performed on the house shows it to have 0.65 ACH50 airtightness, which is close to the 0.60 ACH50 required to be certified a Passive House (see sidebar on facing page). The propane stove in the living area supplements heat on especially cold Vermont days. Enough photovoltaic panels were installed to allow the house to reach almost net zero performance.

Cindy says her favorite things about the house are the compact size, abundance of natural light, large windows that provide great views, and the ease of cleaning and maintaining the house.

# TESTING AIRTIGHTNESS WITH A BLOWER DOOR TEST

The envelope, walls, ceiling, and foundation of a house should be airtight to avoid air leakage from the interior and seepage of outside air to the interior. Airtightness is an important factor in keeping a house comfortable, avoiding high energy costs, and keeping the air quality favorable.

A blower door test is a diagnostic tool used to measure the airtightness of a structure and to show where the leaks in the envelope of the house are. Results of this test can determine if there are leaks in the air sealing, which can then be amended. This test is required for certain certification programs, including ENERGY STAR and Passive House (Passivhaus).

Passive House (PH) has the most stringent blower door test requirements, allowing a maximum infiltration of 0.6 air changes per hour (ACH) when measured at 50 pascals. (Pascals are a measure of pressure.) For reference, typical new houses will test between 4 to 6 ACH at 50 pascals, and typical existing houses will test between 8 to 10 ACH at 50 pascals. Results below 2.0 ACH at 50 pascals may be considered "tight," while 1.0 ACH at 50 pascals is a typical target for high-performance new construction.

When a home is built very tightly, with minimal air leakage, a heat recovery ventilator (HRV) or energy recovery ventilator (ERV) is generally recommended to bring fresh air into the house. These units exchange stale heated or cool air with fresh air in order to keep the house comfortable and healthy for its inhabitants.

# THIMBLEBERRY HOUSE

## KIT HOUSE

**PHOTOGRAPHER**
Lacy Landre
(www.landre.com)

**ARCHITECT/MANUFACTURER**
Lindal Cedar Homes
(https://lindal.com)

**BUILDER**
Shaw Builders
(www.shawbuilders.com)

**INTERIOR DESIGN**
Angela Westmore, LLC
(www.westmoredesignbuild.com)

**SIZE**
1,934 square feet

**LOCATION**
Door County, Wisconsin

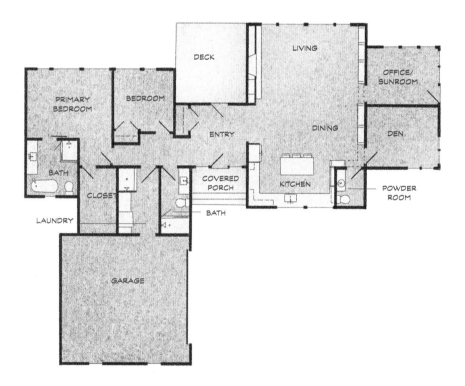

The homeowner, Dr. Judi Tilghman, lives in Chicago, and makes the four-hour drive to this home almost every weekend. She previously owned a log cabin in the area built in 1980 with a Northwoods feel, but she was ready for a new house and a new style. She was planning to purchase another house in the area, but when the pandemic hit she decided to build her own home instead.

**Below:** The exterior is board and batten composite siding with a metal roof. The garage has carriage house-style swing-out doors in metal with a composite overlay.

## GREEN FEATURES
- Metal roof with recycled materials
- Quartz countertops

## ENERGY FEATURES
- Tankless water heater
- High performance insulation
- Air sealing
- Energy recovery ventilator (ERV)
- Ceiling fans

## BUILDING WITH A KIT HOME

Tilghman became familiar with Lindal Cedar Homes when a friend sent her an article about the company in Dwell and she was attracted to their contemporary designs. The parts of the house were prefabricated by Lindal Cedar Homes and built by Greg Shaw, who has been building with them for thirty years. He prefers working with kit houses prefabricated by Lindal rather than traditional site-building because most of the lumber comes precut and a lot of waste is avoided. Lindal also provides architectural help so clients don't have to find an outside designer. Although Shaw has built this model in the past, this homeowner made some changes to the design to meet her lifestyle, choosing such amenities as a dog wash area, a powder room accessed from the great room rather than the kitchen, and a den and an office/sunroom off the living room. She also added a wall of built-in, glass-fronted bookshelves in the living room to house her collection of art, magazines, and books. The house took ten months to complete.

**Opposite:** The homeowner had custom cabinetry installed in the living room. The sectional sofa is 1970s vintage De Sede from Switzerland.

**Below:** The dining table, which also serves as a ping pong table, was designed and built by a custom furniture/iron works shop in Milwaukee. The coffee table, dining room benches, and chairs were all designed by Fernando Cuevas of Flipping Design.

**Above:** The headboard, side tables, and chairs in the primary bedroom are vintage George Nakashima pieces, whose live-edge furniture inspired the tree theme of the house.

## BUILDING AN ENERGY EFFICIENT AND HEALTHY HOME

Shaw went to great lengths to make this house energy efficient, which was a priority for the homeowner. He used high efficiency blow-in-blanket (BIBS) insulation made from a proprietary fabric and fiberglass blowing wool, which according to the company is non-combustible, contains no added formaldehyde, is made with 25 percent or greater recycled content, and attains a high R-value*, substantially reducing air infiltration and thus lowering energy costs. It also helps control noise and is durable. The home fully meets code and is now rated to withstand over 200-mile-an-hour winds.

Shaw carefully identified points throughout the house where there was likely to be air leakage, from the attic to the basement and crawl spaces, and then sealed them up. Since the house was created so airtight, a ventilation system was required to bring in fresh air. An energy recovery ventilator (ERV) was added, which exchanges the stale inside air with fresh outside air while maintaining the temperature already created inside. This also helps with moisture evacuation and the

*R-value: The measure of thermal resistance to heat flow through a given insulating material. The higher the R-value of a material, the greater the insulating effectiveness.

elimination of pollutants and reduces the risk of mold and mildew.

A tankless water heater provides hot water on demand. With storage water heaters, energy is wasted while maintaining the water temperature at a certain level even when hot water is not being used.

**Below, left:** The white cabinetry contrasts with the gold tile backsplash, bronze cabinet hardware, and custom light fixtures over the counter. The farmhouse sink is in keeping with the classic barn profile of the home. White appliances add a modern touch to an otherwise retro style.

**Below, right:** The desk area is off the open living space and was added to the original Lindal Ash design.

## CREATING A UNIQUE DESIGN

Tilghman was clear when she started furnishing her home that she didn't want it to be "the typical Northwoods vacation home with lots of wood and stone." She wanted a light-filled, open design with lots of color and a playful feel. She prefers artisan and vintage items over traditional furnishings. Interior designer Angela Westmore of Milwaukee, Wisconsin, worked with Tilghman on most of the interior finishes, product specifications, the kitchen design, bookshelves, some layouts, and she purchased custom-made accent pieces such as bar stools, towel bars, hooks from artists on Etsy, and handmade pendant lights.

Tilghman says the best things about her house is its openness. Large windows, the flow of the house, its one-floor living, and the unique interior design has the playfulness she was seeking. To increase the sleeping area for guests she installed a Murphy bed with a sofa in the office and a pull-out sofa in the den. And although the house has a small footprint, she says it feels very spacious.

**Left:** The homeowner has two large dogs and loves the dog wash area as part of the laundry room. It has a hand shower, playful dog tail hooks, large knobs on the cabinets, and a stone pebble look in the dog wash. Walnut base cabinetry has a pullout for dog food and bowls at the bottom.

**Right, top:** There is a freestanding bathtub and a floor-mounted faucet in the primary bathroom.

**Below, left:** The decorative table and lamp are in the office, located just off the living room..

**Below, right:** The entry hall opens to the common areas on the right and the bedrooms on the left.

# KIT HOUSES

Kit houses have a long history going back to the late 1800s and early 1900s, when people were purchasing houses from catalogs such as Sears, Roebuck and Company and Aladdin Ready Cut houses. These were delivered by train and often put together by the owner. The parts would be cut in a factory, numbered, and installed on-site. Interestingly, many of these kit houses are still standing.

The concept of delivering all parts of the house was excellent then and is still a practical method of prefabrication. By manufacturing in a conditioned space, the house will be built without having the parts weathered by outside conditions. Parts cut with automated and sophisticated machinery are also built to high standards that cannot always be achieved on-site.

Unlike some other types of prefab construction, the kit package can easily be shipped all over the United States and around the world. Cranes are not required to erect the house, as with some other types of prefab, which reduces the cost of construction. Kit houses are more environmentally friendly than on-site built homes since many of the materials can be recycled with cutoffs from one house used on another.

Lindal Cedar Homes, the company that designed this house, provides many of the materials to build the house. Lindal provides framing, posts and beams, windows, doors, hardware, trim, exterior siding, and some other items. They don't provide foundation work, flooring, roofing, or plumbing. Some parts that are shipped are already connected. The windows are prehung and often mulled together, meaning two or more windows are joined together. The doors are prehung and most of the beams are precut. Numbers are stamped into the lumber to match the plans. Engineering is complete, and all the shell building materials can be shipped in one or two shipments, which saves time and money. Lindal provides a Lifetime Structural Warranty to their clients.

Clients can order from a list of homes, and even make minor changes. Companies such as Lindal can ship these parts more quickly because they have already been predesigned and pre-engineered. Because the time for items such as windows, special doors, and many other products to arrive has increased in recent times, Lindal has the advantage of making several shipments on a timely basis so that even if some items are delayed, the construction is not. Longer lead-time items can be planned to arrive when the builder is ready for them.

All Lindal homes are post and beam construction, and since the exterior walls are load bearing, there is no need for many central structural components.

This house was unique in that rather than multiple beams, there is one central beam that goes through the center of the house and meets the design aesthetic of the owner.

Kit housing has come a long way from the early days when kits were sold in catalogs.

**Below:** There are multiple outdoor seating areas at the rear and side of the house, which also includes a firepit. The property is situated on a one-acre lot, and the whole yard is fenced with a custom-built cedar fence for her two large dogs.

# OLIVE PASSIVE
# HOUSE
### PANELIZED

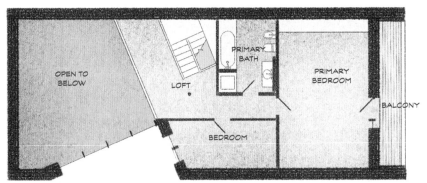

SECOND FLOOR

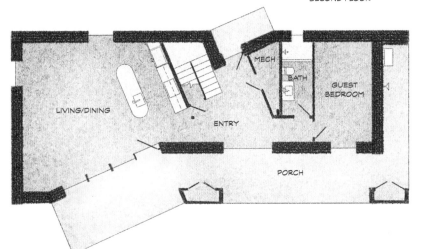

**PHOTOGRAPHER**
Chaunte Vaughn (www.chauntevaughn.
com), unless otherwise noted

**ARCHITECT**
Alessandro Ronfini, DEMO Architects
(https://demoarch.com)

**MANUFACTURER/CONTRACTOR/PHIUS RATER**
Owen O'Connor, Threshold Builders

**SIZE**
1,484 square feet

**LOCATION**
Ulster County, New York

**Opposite:** The deck railing on the east side of the house was designed using the same Siberian larch as the siding. The same details were used on the inside and outside balconies to visually connect the two: one looking toward the landscape, the other overlooking the living room. The balconies were designed to be prefabricated off-site in three parts each and to be installed with no visible fasteners.

Architect Alessandro Ronfini and his wife, Astrid Chastka, an art director and set designer, were ready to get out of their small apartment in Brooklyn and build a house in an area surrounded by nature and lots of open space. The beautiful woodsy lot they selected was just two hours from their business in Brooklyn and located in an artsy upstate New York community. According to Alessandro, their goal was "to create a simple, elemental shape, and then carve this simple volume, almost sculpting it to create a design that fit in the context of the site and responded to the requirements of Passive House."

## GREEN FEATURES

- Locally sourced materials
- Energy recovery ventilator (ERV) system
- Roof with recycled metal
- Salvaged items
- Induction stove

## ENERGY FEATURES

- Super-insulated walls and roof
- Optimal orientation
- Dense-packed cellulose insulation using 85 percent recycled content
- Triple-pane windows
- A single mini-split heat pump to heat and cool the entire home
- Exterior sunshades to reduce heat gain in the summertime

## AIR TIGHTNESS

- 0.26 ACH50

## CERTIFICATIONS

- PHIUS+ 2018
- ENERGY STAR
- Indoor Air Plus

**Right:** The removed "sculpted" volume, which is Siberian larch, contrasts with the large, very solid, black metal mass that covers most of the rest of the siding.

The house is angled south to maximize the solar heat gain in the wintertime and reduce the need for heating, while providing views to a beautiful pond on the southeast. To frame the view toward the pond, catch as much light as possible, and avoid looking toward a neighboring house, Alessandro decided to rotate the main windows on the south to frame the view of the pond. Along this rotated axis are several important components of the house including the main entrance, the stairs, the loft, and the glass wall.

## DESIGNING A HIGHLY ENERGY EFFICIENT HOUSE

Alessandro has lots of experience designing energy efficient houses, but his own house was the first that has been certified Passive House. Even though the house is not energy independent, because of its efficient design, the energy cost of maintaining this house is at least 70 percent less than most existing houses of the same size. This efficiency was accomplished with optimal orientation of the house on the property, highly efficient insulation, triple-pane windows, and a high efficiency HVAC system. A blower door test showed the air tightness to be 0.26, exceeding the Passive House requirement of 0.6 at 50 pascals (see sidebar on page 17).

**Below:** At the rear of the house is a covered patio and a wall of glass, allowing for great views of the pond just beyond.

**Opposite:** The ground floor concrete foundation of the house, with high efficiency insulation on the underside, also serves as the flooring on the first floor. The finish was hand troweled, but not polished.

**Above:** The panels were lifted with a crane onto the prepared foundation. The panels are insulated with dense-packed cellulose, a material containing up to 90 percent recycled content (which is mostly paper.) Photograph courtesy of Seamus McCance.

## CHOOSING TO BUILD WITH PREFABRICATED PANELS

According to Alessandro, using a panelized system allows for the application of insulation and air sealant in a weather-controlled environment. This substantially reduces the risk of failure of glues, sealant, and tapes and provides the perfect conditions for the installation of dense-packed cellulose insulation without the risk of it getting wet. The construction time is not necessarily shorter, but it is less dependent on weather since a large portion of the work happens in an indoor factory.

The quality and precision of the manufacturing of the walls and a precise control of the moisture content of the insulation were essential for the success of the project in the long term. Reducing the site work was also a great benefit but not as crucial in a relatively mild climate like New York where jobsites are active year-round.

Alessandro says, "My house was an experiment and a proof of concept, trying to demonstrate that prefabrication does not necessarily mean square boxes. Even an unusual shape with angles, nooks, and no roof overhangs can be prefabricated, greatly improving the quality of the wall assemblies and reducing the work on-site."

**Left:** The sculpted-out section of the house contains the main entrance to the house, with the living room and kitchen just beyond.

**Below, left:** The bathroom on the second floor has muted mellow tones, with just a touch of red in the light fixture.

**Below, right**: Astrid did most of the work furnishing the guest bathroom. The pink vintage sink was her inspiration for the rest of the bathroom. The couple purchased the sink before they even broke ground for the construction. A friend of the couple welded the white stand to the basin, and then the couple selected inexpensive colorful tiles to complement it. The tap and shower head were custom painted dark red. The sconces are from Alessandro's favorite vintage store in Treviso, Italy, and were brought back in their suitcase after their last pre-pandemic vacation.

**Opposite:** The space on the upper level is currently Alessandro's workspace but their plan is to move his work area out to the garage or to another building on the property (yet to be built) and turn this upper level into a television/relaxation area, with a pull-out couch when friends and family come to visit.

## CREATING A HEALTHY ENVIRONMENT

Like all certified Passive Houses, this house has an energy recovery ventilator (ERV). This ventilation system constantly extracts stale air from the house and replaces it with fresh, filtered air from the exterior. In the process, it uses the energy embodied in the stale air to heat the outdoor air, thus dramatically reducing the need for a powerful heating system.

**Above, top:** This simple shaped, generally monochromatic structure contrasts with the leafy bucolic surroundings.

**Above, bottom:** The Standing-seam metal roofing and siding add a clean modern look to the house as well as provide a sustainable, low maintenance protective envelope.

## BUILDING BY YOURSELF AND WITH FRIENDS

The demand for labor in the area skyrocketed with the onset of the pandemic, making it difficult for the couple to find craftspeople to complete parts of the construction. The couple had to do more of the work than they had planned. With the help of friends, they assembled the kitchen, built the island, installed the wood floor on the upper level, and installed all the wood siding on the exterior. Alessandro says that although it took much more time than they anticipated, along with some stress and hard work, it was a fun time and a great learning experience.

Alessandro loves how quiet and peaceful the house is. With such excellent insulation, even if a truck comes down the driveway, they can hardly hear it. He and Astrid particularly love the light in the living room, which is bright and vivid in the mornings and diffuse and calm in the afternoons.

The house was awarded the Best Project by a Young Professional at the 2021 Passive House Institute US (PHIUS) Conference.

# EXTERIOR RETRACTABLE SHADES AND BLINDS

Exterior solar shades are more effective at reducing heat than interior shades because they filter the heat before it has a chance to enter the house, keeping interiors noticeably cooler. Interior solar shades protect occupants from heat by radiation, but they do not prevent the heating of the interior environment itself, thus doing little to reduce the energy needed to cool a space. The Olive Passive House has exterior solar shades. Alessandro says they only use the shades in the summertime to reduce glare and limit the need for air-conditioning. Although the trees do most of the work in blocking the sun in the summertime, the shades also reduce the glare on computer screens. The shades used here are motorized with radio remote control. They can also be paired with home automation, or they can have optional wind, rain, sun sensors, and timers to raise and lower them. The shades on this house are only visible when lowered. When raised, they sit entirely behind the roofline.

Exterior shades are available in a variety of fabrics and constructions. Fabrics range from transparent solar shades in different densities, to clear vinyl that protect against cold and rain, to blackout total privacy fabrics, very popular for hot tub areas. The wind load of the shade is an important consideration, therefore influencing the type of construction. The solar shades in the Olive Passive House were from North Solar Screen.

Also available are retractable exterior aluminum blinds that come in a wide variety of colors and designs. These blinds allow the house to receive natural light and the view even when the blinds are tilted to block the sun. They are available motorized and connected to a smart automation system, which can be synced with sensors to adjust the position of the blinds and the angle of the slats to keep the maximum light inside the home, while preventing heat from coming in. During freezing weather, when ice might block the shades, an alert can be sent to the blinds to not move during that time. Although these blinds are not yet popular in the US, Europeans have been using them for more than sixty years. For further information about these blinds, see www.cphba.com.

# THE PASSIVE NARROWTIVE

## STRUCTURAL INSULATED PANELS (SIPS)

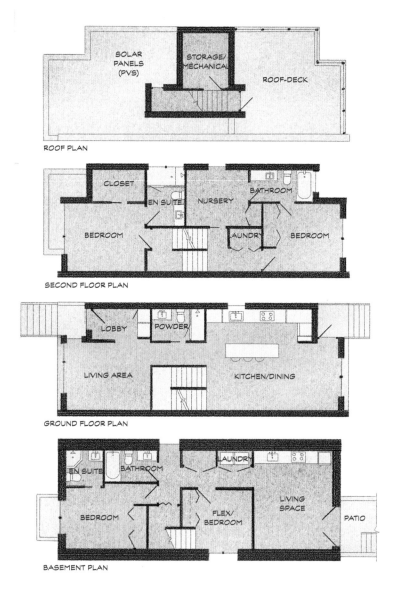

ROOF PLAN

SECOND FLOOR PLAN

GROUND FLOOR PLAN

BASEMENT PLAN

**PHOTOGRAPHER**
Martin Knowles
(www.mkphotomedia.com)

**ARCHITECT**
Nick Bray Architecture
(https://nickbray.ca)

**BUILDER**
JDL/Black Thumb Contracting
(http://www.jdlhomesvancouver.com)
(https://www.blackthumbcontracting.com)

**MANUFACTURER**
Primer SIPs
(www.premiersips.com)

**SIZE**
Primary House 1,790 square feet
Tenant Suite 860 square feet

**LOCATION**
Vancouver, British Columbia, Canada

**Opposite:** The exterior of the house is a combination of hardwood and highly sustainable fiber cement siding. The large front windows provide significant solar gain in the winter. The solar-shading canopies, along with the tree at the front of the house, block the sun on hot summer days.

Architect Nick Bray found a small lot in a family-friendly neighborhood in central Vancouver that was affordable because of the many challenges of building on it. He was motivated to demonstrate how a highly efficient, sustainable home can be built on what many would consider an undesirable lot. Bray wanted to prove he could build a Certified Passive House on this small, narrow,

## GREEN FEATURES

- Low/zero volatile organic compounds (VOC) products
- Electric car charger
- Recycled materials
- Low-flow fixtures
- Water-conserving washing machine and dishwasher
- Locally sourced materials
- Seismically upgraded
- Native plantings requiring minimal water
- Rainwater collection used for the garden
- Induction stove

## ENERGY FEATURES

- Photovoltaic panels
- Heat pump water heater
- Heat pump heating/cooling
- Large canopies
- Stack effect
- LED lights
- Heat recovery ventilators (HRVs) (93 percent efficient)
- Concrete floors for thermal mass
- Automated reflective blinds
- SIPs
- Electric radiant heating
- Eco-friendly, spray-on air barrier exterior membrane
- Insulated concrete form foundation (ICF)
- High efficiency windows

## AIRTIGHTNESS

- 0.3 ACH

## CERTIFICATION

- Passive House Canada (PH)

challenging site, while creating an efficient house design. He also looked forward to testing innovative products and technology. He hopes this house will motivate others to rebuild crumbling houses and to invigorate local struggling neighborhoods.

Bray designed this house for his young family and an additional garden suite below for tenants, using the most innovative, energy efficient, sustainable, and healthy materials available. The house was designed to be flexible so that the current configuration can be adapted to changing needs. Currently Bray's family occupies the main house which consists of three bedrooms. The lower suite has two bedrooms. However, the main house can be modified to have four bedrooms with the lower suite becoming one bedroom or some other configuration, depending on their situation. One of Bray's major considerations was to maximize the use of space for now and in the future.

## MEETING WITH CONSTRUCTION CHALLENGES

Bray chose to build on this lot even though it was on a "peat bog." A peat bog is a type of wet marshland which stores a large amount of carbon due to the accumulated deposits of various types of dead plant material. These peat bogs need to remain in the ground so as not to contribute to climate change. Bray says it was like "building on a sponge." For him to build on this property, he had to devise a complex foundation plan using forty-six 40-foot piles in the ground.

The house could also only be 18 feet wide and 48 feet deep on this narrow lot, making it a design and energy challenge. The south side of most buildings provide the most light and solar energy, which in this case was only 18 feet wide. To keep the house light filled, Bray designed the house with large windows, tall ceilings, and an open-tread staircase allowing natural light to penetrate deep into the home.

**Opposite:** The small niche near the front entrance provides a sitting area. A short hallway connects the living room with the powder room, kitchen/dining area, and den. The main floor has concrete flooring that stores solar gain and provides additional sound/fire buffering between the main house and the tenant suite. (See sidebar on page 57.)

**Below:** Large windows provide natural lighting throughout the year. Although the steam fireplace in the living room provides no heat, it is visually appealing and nonpolluting.

**Above:** The sitting area just off the kitchen and dining area is a great play area for the couple's children.

## BUILDING WITH STRUCTURAL INSULATED PANELS AND INSULATED CONCRETE FORMS

Bray chose to build the house using structural insulated panels (SIPs,) which offer excellent airtight insulation. These were used for their high energy efficiency and to speed up the process of building this house, which was drawn-out by the complicated foundation structure. These locally manufactured prefabricated panels were graphite-infused to reflect and absorb thermal radiation, improving the ability of the SIPs to insulate. They were also impregnated with waterproofing to extend the life of the panels.

Insulated concrete forms (ICFs) (see sidebar on page 47) made the foundation and lower level of the house airtight and well insulated. All wall assemblies including the SIPs and ICF were chosen for their high R-value/inch*.

---

*R-value is the measure of thermal resistance to heat flow through a given insulating material. The higher a material's R-value, the greater its insulating effectiveness.

## PASSIVE HOUSE STANDARDS MET

With Bray's design plan he was able to exceed the airtightness (see sidebar on page 17) required by Passive House Canada, which is 0.6 ACH50. In addition to the airtight foundation and walls, the design added to the efficiency of the structure.

The split-level design and south-facing windows provide solar gain in the winter. The large canopies along with the tree in the front of the house protect it against summer overheating. The concrete floors on the first floor also keep the house cool in the summer and warm in the winter. The automated reflective blinds help to deflect the summer heat, as well as provide privacy. Radiant heating imbedded in the concrete floor helps to maintain a constant temperature in the house.

**Left:** The kitchen and dining room are open to each other. The steps lead to the bedrooms above and the suite below. The open-tread staircase allows natural light to penetrate deep into the home and air to flow between the levels.

**Below:** The kitchen has high efficiency appliances including an induction range and a water-conserving dishwasher.

## BUILDING A SMART HOUSE

The house was designed not only with the most sophisticated heating and ventilation systems, but Bray also made it a very "smart" house. All the light fixtures can be voice activated and automatically turn off when residents leave the house. The bathroom lights are controlled by movement sensors.

**Left:** The shower in the primary bathroom is barrier free.

**Below:** The primary bedroom has a walk-in closet and en suite bathroom. The staircase separates this bedroom from the other two bedrooms and bathroom.

## MAXIMIZING SPACE EFFICIENCY

Because of the small footprint, space efficiency was a major factor in the design. Bray designed the house to be flexible in its configuration, with creative storage space and limited hallways.

To limit the use of hallways Bray devised a clever split-level design plan for the second floor, alternating the height of the bedrooms with the use of stairways, thus eliminating the need for a corridor. The main-level powder room is preplumbed for a future accessible shower to add to the flexibility of the space. The bedroom located at the higher space allowed for a 12-foot ceiling in the living room, making that space feel larger than it is.

With his additional concern for sustainability, Bray designed the house with a strong foundation and excellent materials for the walls and interior. He even seismically upgraded the house to withstand a significant earthquake. Bray says he wants the house to last more than 100 years

The Passive Narrowtive provides proof of concept for a perfect eco-friendly, comfortable, energy efficient home on an available less-than-perfect lot.

**Top, above:** The rooftop garden provides outdoor living space with beautiful views of the North Shore Mountains.

**Above:** Multiple windows allow lots of natural light into this primary bedroom.

**Overleaf:** At the rear of the house is a sitting and dining area, expanding the living space. The entrance to the tenant suite can be seen.

# STACK EFFECT

The stack, or chimney, effect is a natural method of ventilation whereby air moves in and out of buildings through a duct or vertical passageway. Hot air is less dense than cold air and rises due to its low pressure. The rising warm air reduces the pressure at the base of the building, sucking cold air into the space from the outside. This is an excellent natural method of cooling a house, particularly for small houses where HVAC equipment space is more limited. In the Passive Narrowtive, an operable window at the top of the stairs uses the stack effect to naturally ventilate the house.

# PASSIVE HOUSE CERTIFICATION

Passive House Certification is achieved by meeting the standards set up by the nonprofit organization Passive House Institute, or Passivhaus. This standard was first established in Germany but is now being used in many countries around the world, including the United States. (The U.S. has its own arm of the organization [known as Passive House Institute United States, or Phius], as does Canada [PassiveHouse Canada].) It focuses on reducing energy consumption for space heating and cooling by about 80 percent, reducing a structure's ecological footprint as well as on creating a comfortable and affordable home. The Passive House Planning Package (PHPP) software can be used to predict energy usage and losses for individual homes or other structures. The requirements are stringent and include maximum heating and cooling demand, total primary energy consumption, and a maximum leakage (0.06) of air volume per hour at 50 pascals of pressure, which is measured with a blower door test (see sidebar on page 17).

Passive houses are designed with superinsulation, high-performance windows, adequate shading (for warmer months), an airtight building shell or "envelope," and the use of an energy recovery ventilator (ERV) to exchange the interior air with fresh outside air. Creating energy is not the main focus of PH structures, although some houses do include active solar systems. Passive Houses are designed to save approximately 75 percent of the entire energy used in a house compared to average new builds. Any house can be designed to be a Passive House. However, having a house PH certified by a third-party certifier assures the homeowner that the house has met the high standards it was designed to meet.

# COWBOY MODERN
# DESERT ECO-RETREAT

## PREFABRICATED STEEL FRAME

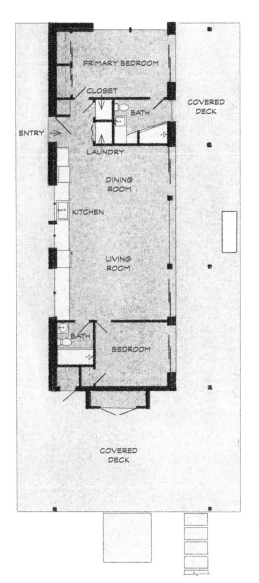

**PHOTOGRAPHER**
Lance Gerber (unless otherwise noted)

**ARCHITECT**
Jeremy Levine Design
(www.jeremylevine.com)

**GENERAL CONTRACTOR**
D&D Construction
(www.ddconstruction.com)

**MANUFACTURER**
Blue Sky Building Systems
(www.blueskybuildingsystems.com)

**SIZE**
1,200 square feet

**LOCATION**
Pioneertown, California

A rchitect Jeremy Levine, his wife Robin, and their two children divide their time between this desert home and their home in Los Angeles.

Jeremy designed this home to be as energy efficient and sustainable as possible. His goal was to design the house to minimize solar gain, capture the beautiful views from every area of the house, and provide plenty of shade to off-set the hot desert heat. All his design decisions were based on building the most eco-friendly home, minimizing its impact on the land, and using the most sustainable materials, such as reclaimed lumber throughout and recycled metal roofing.

The design of this home was inspired by the nearby Old West architecture and the stark desert landscape, combined with modern, minimal design, which Jeremy calls "Cowboy Modernism."

**Below:** The house sits on a 120-acre property, surrounded by mesas, in Southern California's Mojave Desert near Pioneertown and Joshua Tree National Park. When Jeremy purchased the property, it was natural and untouched, accessible only by a dirt road and surrounded by natural washes (dry streambeds that are naturally carved through the desert), huge boulders, and hundreds of Joshua trees.

## GREEN FEATURES

- Reclaimed lumber
- Metal roof with recycled material
- Repurposed galvanized livestock troughs
- Gray water system
- Dual-flush toilet

## ENERGY FEATURES

- Optimal solar orientation
- Large overhangs
- Concrete floors
- Large outdoor spaces
- Ceiling fans
- Cross ventilation
- Wrap-around porch, shading the glazing
- Daylighting
- LED lighting

## BUILDING ON PROTECTED LAND

All construction plans were designed to avoid disturbing this untouched pristine location in the Pipes Canyon of the Mohave Desert. Since the house was to be built in a specially designated Resource Conservation Zone, Levine chose to use a prefabrication construction method, which has a much lower impact on the natural environment, a requirement for construction in this area.

A biological inspection was required before construction could be started to ensure that no desert tortoises or owls would be affected on the site. The Joshua trees also could not be removed.

**Above:** The beautiful site is surrounded by Joshua trees and mesas. Photo courtesy of Jared Fuller.

## CHOOSING A PREFABRICATED METAL FRAME SYSTEM

Jeremy says he opted to use a prefab method of construction because it would speed up the assembly of the house and reduce the size of the construction team and the amount of machinery and trucks needed to access the site.

The beams and columns in this metal frame system are made from light gauge Galvalume that can easily be carried and lifted into place by one or two workers—unlike solid lumber of the same size, which is very heavy and requires more labor. All the precut and predrilled metal components were bolted together on-site with no welding required. Jeremy says that even the cleanup was easier because there were no cut-off wood pieces. Everything was precisely cut and drilled off-site, and the bolts were pretested to fit for accurate connections.

The entire structure was assembled in just three days, with no material waste, unlike houses that are fully constructed on-site. Jeremy concludes that there were big savings in time, labor, waste, and impact on the land using this system.

**Below, top:** The metal framing of the house was prefabricated off-site, brought to the site, and bolted together. Photo courtesy of Jeremy Levine.

**Below, bottom:** The floor-to-ceiling glass doors were designed to fill the house with light and cross ventilation. The concrete floor provides thermal mass, capturing the warmth of the sun and releasing it in the cooler evenings. Ceiling fans supplement cooling during the hot days.

## PASSIVE LIGHTING AND VENTILATION

The placement and orientation of the house were designed to capture the natural breezes that flow through the canyon and minimize solar heat gain. Every room has sliding glass doors to admit light and breezes, supplemented by large cooling fans. Openings on both sides of the main spaces are aligned so the wind moves directly across the house, unimpeded by walls.

The large porch roof wraps around the house, providing shade, which lowers the temperature in the house by as much as 10 degrees. These large exterior shaded parts of the house are equal in size to the interior space, vastly extending the living space of the house.

Passive daylighting fills the interior of the house, eliminating the need for artificial light during the day. Clerestory windows wash the ceiling with reflected light rather than direct sunlight into the open space.

## BUILDING IN THIS DESERT LOCATION

There were many challenges in building the house at a 4,800-foot altitude with its extremes in weather conditions. Jeremy says choosing the right materials and details were critical to optimal performance under these conditions. He chose a steel frame because, unlike wood, metal does not expand and contract significantly as the temperature changes. Reclaimed lumber was chosen because its moisture content is minimal and will not expand and contract with extreme heat and cold, unlike new lumber. A clear sealant was applied to augment the wood's weather resistance.

**Opposite:** Large glass windows and doors connect the homeowners visually and physically to the dramatic landscape while allowing soothing cross breezes and natural light to flood the interiors. The wood ceiling, like the other wood used in the construction, is reclaimed Douglas fir lumber.

**Above:** The bedrooms off the sides of the common area have multiple windows to provide ample natural light and ventilation. This primary bedroom opens to the front of the house.

**Right:** The cabinetry and shelves in the bathroom are built with reclaimed wood.

## MECHANICALLY PROVIDING HEATING AND COOLING

This part of the desert, known as the high desert because of its altitude, gets very cold at night and can also snow during the winter. A high efficiency HVAC system was installed to help control the indoor comfort with these vast variations in temperature. To improve the efficiency of the HVAC system, all the ducting for the heating and cooling was placed inside of the conditioned space of the house, rather than in an uncooled attic. This system will be powered by solar panels installed on the roof.

**Above:** A stepped path leads to a hot spa and a cold cowboy tub, a nod to the Old West tradition of repurposing galvanized livestock troughs.

**Right:** The many windows and doors on all areas of the house provide natural ventilation and light as well as easy access to the outdoors.

**Above:** The roof overhangs form a shaded wrap-around deck as large as the indoor part of the house. The covered area provides space for grilling, dining, and lounging. The fire table on the front porch was designed by Jeremy Levine Design and is made from leftover home-construction materials.

## BUILDING WITH RECYCLED MATERIALS

All lumber used in the construction is reclaimed to both conserve resources and blend in with the landscape.

The metal roof is composed of 25 percent recycled content. Because of its durability it can last up to 50 percent longer than a standard roof, while using the materials more efficiently. The roof also has a special coating that has high solar reflectance making it a "cool roof."

Jeremy states, "The Cowboy Modern Desert Eco-Retreat is just that—a place of respite for my young family and friends, where they can enjoy open views and an unpolluted night sky. Working remotely takes on new meaning here."

# CONCRETE FLOORS FOR THERMAL MASS

Concrete flooring is growing in popularity in large part because of its low maintenance and stylish look. However, another major reason for using this flooring is the thermal mass created by the concrete. Thermal mass is generally solid matter (although it can also be liquid) that can absorb and store warmth and coolness. Concrete, brick, and stone are examples of high-density materials that can store and release energy back into a space. Flooring with a high thermal mass can help to heat and cool the interior space. In winter, the solar energy is stored during the day and released at night when the air temperature drops in the house, thus reducing the energy required to heat the interior space. During the summer, heat is absorbed by the solid surfaces, keeping the space more comfortable during the day and reducing the need for air-conditioning.

Concrete floors can be less expensive than wood floors if the foundation is slab-on-grade. They are also highly durable, fire resistant, slip resistant, and eco-friendly. A variety of stains and paints can also create a unique flooring look. Concrete flooring is ideal for radiant floor heating systems because of their great thermal conducting ability. The main issue with concrete is that it absorbs moisture, so the floors need to be properly sealed. They are also hard underfoot and generally cold. Although concrete floors may not work particularly well with traditional décor, they have become increasing popular with many new contemporary designed homes.

# HARRISON LANE HOUSE
## STRUCTURAL INSULATED PANELS (SIPS)

**PHOTOGRAPHER**
Brett Hitchens
(www.brettryanstudios.com)

**DESIGNER/BUILDER/INTERIOR DESIGNER**
Lanefab Design/Build
(www.lanefab.com)

**SIZE**
940 square feet

**LOCATION**
Vancouver, BC, Canada

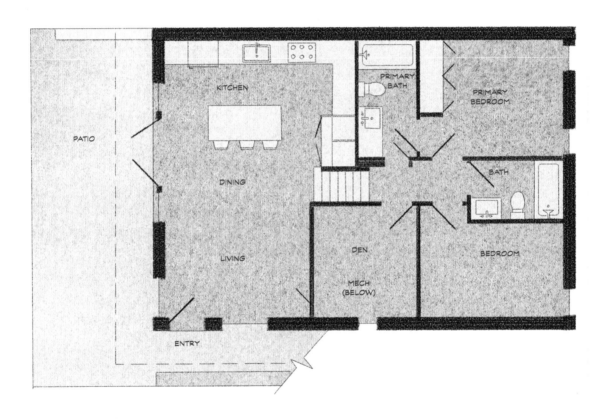

Virginia and Thomas owned a 550-square-foot condo in Richmond and were looking to upgrade to a larger home in either Richmond or nearby Vancouver. However, they found the larger condos were too expensive. Luckily, Thomas's parents owned a house on a large piece of land where there was room for them to build a laneway house or accessible dwelling unit (ADU).

**Below:** The Harrison Lane House opens to the lane where the garage would be. According to Bryn Davidson of LaneFab, "The shape of the home is unique because of the slope of the property, with the floors stepping down from the lane to the yard, and the slope of the roof following the slope of the land. Because the lane house is higher than the main house and the lot is very long, the patio and French doors have a view out and beyond the main house, which is quite different from the typical laneway house, where the yard is more like a contained courtyard."

## GREEN FEATURES
- Quartz countertops

## ENERGY FEATURES
- Structural insulated panels (SIPs)
- Triple-glazed windows and doors
- Heat recovery ventilation
- High efficiency washer/dryer
- Radiant floor heating
- No air conditioning

## SELECTING A BUILDER

The couple started researching construction options to build on the property, talking to various construction companies to educate themselves on the process and the cost.

They chose LaneFab to build their home because, unlike many other companies, LaneFab offered an all-inclusive package, which meant they secured the permits and handled all the site work, including the foundation, sewer and water connections, pathways, landscaping, and retaining walls.

LaneFab was also a perfect option because of their vast experience building laneway houses; they are aware of all the legalities and information needed to complete the home. In addition, LaneFab offers a customized plan, which the couple preferred to a pre-designed one. The couple had not considered building with prefab components until they met with the LaneFab representative. They were impressed with the efficiency they could get with structural insulated panels.

The couple initially hoped to build a 1,200-square foot home, but due to city bylaws their home could only be 950 square feet. Virginia says the two-bedroom, two-bathroom (plus a den) house works for them since the ceilings are high and the house feels bigger than it is. They hope to one day build a small loft in the children's bedroom. With the cost of real estate in Vancouver, building this laneway house was their best option, since they did not have to purchase the property.

**Opposite:** A small café table in the open common area provides an alternate eating area to the island counter.

**Below:** The kitchen is very white except for the colorful geometric tiled backsplash. The countertop is quartz. The large kitchen island doubles as the dining table and comes in handy when hosting small parties.

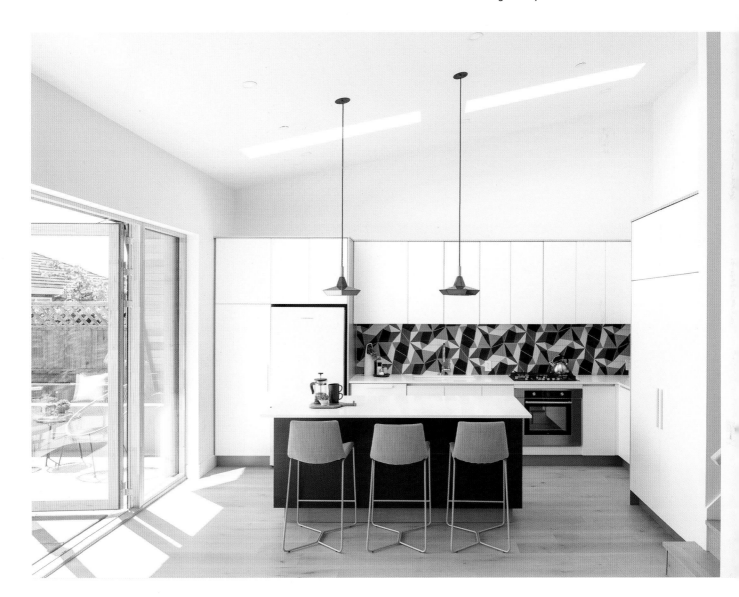

**Left, top:** The flooring throughout is engineered hardwood that has radiant heating. The living room opens to a large porch through French doors.

**Left, bottom:** The primary bedroom is lit by two large windows, which are high on the wall for privacy.

**Opposite, top:** The second bedroom (after this photo) became a nursery when their baby was born.

**Opposite, bottom:** The primary bathroom has a skylight that makes the room naturally bright. Some of Virginia's favorite aspects of the house are the rose gold hardware, rain shower faucet, and the custom cabinetry. Like most of the house, the bathroom is mostly white except for the cabinetry and the colorful tiles.

## UNCERTAIN COMPLETION TIMES

The couple signed contracts to start construction in late 2018 and they expected the process to take a year. They were lucky to get into a pilot laneway house program and their permit process was expedited. However, the early arrival of the permits was offset by the construction team not being ready with a crew to build so quickly. There were also soil issues and then the COVID-19 pandemic hit, and everything slowed down. They ended up moving in April 2020.

## THE DESIGN PROCESS

When they began the design process, energy efficiency was not their priority, except for the financial aspects. In retrospect, they say it would be much more important to them now. They appreciate the triple-paned windows which LaneFab recommended. Thomas was insistent on having lots of natural light and really wanted large skylights in the kitchen. They also wanted to have three bedrooms, since they plan for this to be their forever home.

The couple wanted a mid-century modern feel, which they achieved with the slanted metal roof, clean lines, and colorful tiles in the kitchen and bathrooms. They opted to use Canadian companies as much as possible; their light fixtures are Canadian, along with their appliances.

Their home ended up about $50,000 over budget because of an issue with the foundation and the need to rebuild all the retaining walls on the property. "We still believe that our house was worth it, as even with the extra cost we could not buy a property nearly as nice for even twice what we paid to build it."

# WHAT ARE STRUCTURAL INSULATED PANELS (SIPS)?

SIPs are energy efficient, make homes more comfortable, and can be installed quickly, which explains why this construction method is growing in popularity. Most SIPs are sandwiches of rigid insulation (molded polystyrene [MPS] or expanded polystyrene [EPS]) structurally bonded between two structural oriented strand boards (OSB) or plywood panels. Some are available with metal in place of boards. Panels join using long, interlocking strips of wood, called splines, to create an airtight barrier for roofing, siding, or flooring. Since the panels are factory manufactured to each floor plan, routed channels, or chases, are cut into the panels for electricians to easily install wiring and cables. Window and door openings are generally cut out of the panels in the factory. Insulated structural headers (for large window and door spans) and cabinetry are also manufactured for each home plan in the factory.

After precision factory fabrication, SIPs are delivered by truck to the building site for installation. Large panels are usually hoisted into place with the help of a lift or crane, and smaller panels can be easily lifted by hand and secured by one or two people. Houses can be designed using Autocad®, and the panels are cut using a computer-run machine or computer numerical control (CNC) machine. The numbered panels are quickly erected on-site.

# LANEWAY HOUSES DEFINED

The term "laneway house" generally refers to a small residential structure built behind an existing home on a lot and which has the front entrance opening to the back alleyway, or lane, rather than the street. They are in the category of traditional accessory dwelling units (ADUs). The earliest modern laneway house were built in Canada in the late 1980s and early 1990s. They did not become popular in Canada until 2009 when the Municipal Government of Vancouver passed a new rezoning law permitting laneway houses on all residential properties. The popularity of laneway houses in Canada seemed to spark interest in ADUs in the United States, where various states and municipalities are allowing their construction. Like all other ADUs, laneway houses add density in a location without the construction of large buildings that may change the nature of the area.

**Below:** The French doors leading to the exterior are one of the couple's favorite aspects of their home.

# GOOD VIBES HOUSE

## MODULAR

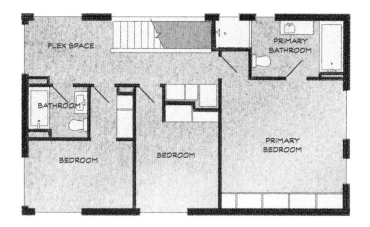

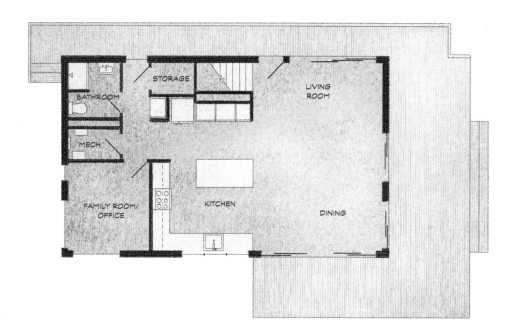

**PHOTOGRAPHER**
Gordon Scott

**ARCHITECT/GENERAL CONTRACTOR/ MANUFACTURER**
Connect Homes
(https://connect-homes.com)

**SIZE**
1,920 square feet

**LOCATION**
Los Angeles, California

**Opposite:** The dark gray and black exterior contrasts with the light, bright interior. The couple says the numerous floor-to-ceiling windows and sliding glass doors let in an abundance of natural light along with generous airflow, reducing the need for air-conditioning during warmer months.

In 2007, Michelle and Brian Duff bought a small 1940s home in West Los Angeles. After ten years, two children, and two dogs, the family outgrew their small house. They knew they had to rebuild their home or move to something a bit more functional for their

## GREEN FEATURES

- Dual-flush/low-flow toilets
- Low-flow faucets and shower head
- High efficiency dishwasher
- Rain catchment system
- Tankless water heater

## ENERGY FEATURES

- LED lights
- Mini-split heat pumps
- High performance aluminum doors/windows
- ENERGY STAR appliances
- Daylighting
- Cross ventilation

family. Because they adored their neighborhood, they decided to knock down the current house and build one at that location—a house that would better meet their changing needs.

Even though this house is not large, it is bigger than their previous home and has plenty of room for the family. "It provides everything that we need without waste, and it opens seamlessly to our outdoor space, so it always feels very open and spacious," Michelle says.

## BUILDING MODULAR

After becoming interested in the concept of pre-fab construction, the couple researched several companies, and were most drawn to Connect's designs. Only *after* reaching out to Connect, did they realize that one of the cofounders, Jared Levy, is the son of a woman who rented them a home in Santa Monica for several years. They saw this as a positive sign that they had selected the right company.

The couple believed building prefab was a positive decision because of the efficiency of materials and labor. Getting the house built quickly was also a consideration so that the disruption to their lives and to the other people in the neighborhood was minimized.

**Opposite and below:** The common areas are open to each other and have large windows and sliding glass doors, making the interior and exterior seamless.

**Above and left:** All of the appliances in the kitchen are ENERGY STAR rated in line with the couple's desire to keep the house very energy efficient.

**Opposite, top:** At the top of the stairs is a small seating area for reading or just enjoying the view.

**Opposite, bottom:** The primary bedroom has massive windows allowing in lots of light and also has a door opening up to the back patio.

## GOING THROUGH
## THE DESIGN PHASE

The couple told the design team at Connect Homes their major priorities were to have lots of natural light, easy access to outdoor space, and energy efficiency. And given that the space was limited, the home had to be well designed to provide multifunctional room for the whole family.

While in the design stage the couple also began thinking about the possibility of staying in this home for many, many years or having their parents live or stay with them, if necessary, in the future. To make sure this could be possible, they wanted the first floor living space to be very open so it could easily accommodate assistive devices. They also wanted a bedroom and bathroom on

**Above:** The rear porch extends around two sides of the house and is surrounded by natural foliage.

the first level so that all the necessities of living were available without going upstairs.

The Good Vibes House was built with six modules and set on the site of their old house. They were able to stay in their house for most of that year, while the new house was designed and produced in the factory. They then moved out of their house for about eight months until the modular house was complete.

The COVID-19 pandemic made them use the space they had for multiple functions: school, exercise, work, family time. The guest room on the main floor serves as an office for Brian, gaming desk for their son, and as a remote classroom for the kids. At the top of the stairs there's a space for reading or relaxing, or for the dogs to keep watch over the neighborhood. The couple are delighted with the simplicity of the design and all the natural light and fresh breezes that come into the house.

Brian says, "The house is uncomplicated and allows us to live that same way. It offers a very functional and clean base that lets us move and live easily, both indoors and out."

# THE ADVANTAGES OF BUILDING MODULAR

Although there are multiple ways of prefabricating a house, modular construction is among the most complete method. Entire modules or boxes are produced in the factory and can quickly be set on a foundation, which can be prepared at the same time as the modules. Unlike most other methods, the house can be closed-up and watertight in a day or two, eliminating the intrusion of rain, snow, and sleet. Keeping the interior dry is advantageous in preventing mold and mildew, as well as hindering the twisting and warping of the wood.

Modular construction is growing in popularity in home construction as well as commercial construction because of how quickly the structures can be erected and the cost savings in building them. Modular manufacturers can purchase materials in bulk, which saves the manufacturer money that they pass on to consumers. There is also far less waste. Cutoffs from one house can be used on the construction of another house and certain materials, such as metal and dry wall, can be recycled. Dumpsters are rarely required on job sites where modular homes are being built. Poor weather conditions will not delay construction since the modules are built in ideal conditions. For many workers the controlled conditions in a factory and working on a regular schedule are preferable to the harsh, sporadic work that occurs with on-site building. People often ask, "If this is such a wonderful way to build, how come all houses aren't built this way?" The answer: Prefab construction is the best kept secret in America.

# ASHFORD WEEHOUSE

## MODULAR

**PHOTOGRAPHER**
Ed Caldwell (unless otherwise noted)
(www.edwardcaldwell.com)

**ARCHITECT**
Geoffrey Warner
Alchemy, LLC
(https://alchemyarch.com)

**MANUFACTURER**
Plant Prefab
(www.plantprefab.com)

**GENERAL CONTRACTOR**
Fondare Finish Construction
(https://fondarefinish.com)

**SIZE**
1,450 square feet (excluding the base)

**LOCATION**
Santa Rosa, California

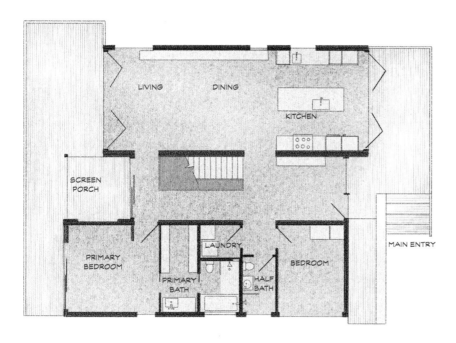

After losing the home they had designed and built in Santa Rosa, California, to the 2017 Tubbs Wildfire, Carol and Will Ashford, although traumatized by losing their home, chose to return to their hillside vista and build a new home there. The couple, along with their son Ryan, recognized the strains of rebuilding in the fire's wake due to the lack and expense of qualified available builders.

**Above:** The three modular units sit on a concrete foundation that houses mechanicals, an art studio, bathroom, storage, and stair landing.

## GREEN FEATURES

- Low flow faucets
- Unpainted steel custom steps
- Natural oil floor coating rather than one with VOCs
- Fire-resistant components

## ENERGY FEATURES

- Passive cooling through ventilating skylights with sun/rain sensors
- South side pergola, which offers sun control and doubles as rack for photovoltaic solar panels (installed after photography)
- Back-up battery for four-day house operation during frequent outages
- White TPO roof for reflecting solar radiation
- Heat recovery ventilator
- Mini-split heat pump
- 2-inch-thick continuous exterior insulation, which provides a critical thermal break for heating and cooling load reductions

They ultimately chose Alchemy to design their home because of Alchemy's experience with sustainable modern design around the country, in addition to their experience with off-site modular construction with Plant Prefab and other high-end factories. As interested and capable artists, the couple were involved in all choices made for their new home and say it was important to be part of the design process for their own healing.

**Opposite and below:** Large bifold glass wall systems and windows provide natural ventilation, daylighting, and beautiful views of the surrounding mountains and natural foliage.

**Right:** The modular units are lifted with a crane and set in place. (Photo courtesy of the owner.)

## THE MODULAR CONSTRUCTION

The modular house was built with three custom "boxes" atop a concrete base, which was poured on-site. The lower level contains mechanicals, a gallery space, storage, and an artist studio with an adjoining bath that can double as a guest room or internal accessory dwelling unit for a live-in aide, allowing them to age in place. The three modular units were sited to maximize northeasterly mountain views, natural ventilation, indoor-outdoor living (despite the difficulties of a steep site), and views throughout the house from north to south.

The first modular is clad in a custom-designed copper metal, created with a brake press that bends metal sheets and creates precise ribbed bands in the metal. That modular contains the kitchen and living and dining rooms. The second module, also in the custom brake pattern, is white-painted steel containing the entry, art gallery, and hall, which expands views and circulation as the core of the house. The third module is also clad in white of the same brake-patterned steel and consists of a primary bedroom, en suite bathroom, guest bedroom, bathroom, and laundry room. The variety of cladding materials brings texture to the site while graphically defining the space.

Inside, simple A-grade maple plywood frames the openings between the modules, concealing the "mating" lines, and helping to celebrate the voids and recesses within the otherwise modest white interior. The outdoors is brought in through windows and glass bifold doors creating walls made of glass. A streamlined interior palette includes plywood accents, exposed stud walls, white cabinetry, slate, and porcelain tile.

**Opposite:** The glass walls allow light to penetrate the house. The glassed-in stairway leads to the lower areas. The artwork was produced by the owners.

**Above:** The white kitchen cabinets and appliances make the area look larger than it is. The minimalist center island kitchen hides an incredible amount of storage and utility yet remains an efficient place for several people to gather and work together.

**Right:** Glazing in all rooms is a major feature of this house.

## PROTECTING THE HOUSE FROM FUTURE FIRES

Although it is impossible to totally prepare for a future fire, steps were taken to make the house more fireproof. The exterior material on the prefab modules is metal, which, although not "fireproof," does act as the critical first layer of defense against flying embers. A continuous, ceramic-faced, fire-resistant sheathing was used in the exterior wall faces behind the siding and ceiling to provide both flame-spread and burn-through resistance. The cantilevered soffits are covered in a fire-resistant, fly-ash concrete composite.

The decking is made from ipe, a high-density hardwood with a class A fire rating. (Class A rated materials do not burn well and are very unlikely to contribute fuel to a fire.) Ipe has a very low flame-spread rating and meets some strict local specifications. The prefab modules sit on a concrete "plinth." Concrete was chosen because it is a noncombustible material, deterring wind-blown embers from igniting the house at the base of the wall. It is also separated by vegetation at grade.

According to architect Warner, "The beauty of this house lies in the simple celebration of the modular boxes and their joinery. The recesses and openings from doors, foyers, skylights, and screens allow the intense local light into the entire house in controlled yet changing ways throughout the course of the day."

**Above:** An open concept and large glazing make the space feel larger than it is. Beautiful views can be seen here from the living and dining areas.

**Left:** The skylight in the hallway brings added light into the house.

# MINI-SPLIT HEAT PUMPS

Mini-split heat pumps have been used around the world for many years. But they have been gaining in popularity in the United States in recent years because of their energy efficiency, size, ease of installation, and the ability to zone the different areas of the house. This house features a traditional but small mini-split ducted system. The ducts are for heat recovery and air distribution. Because of the modest heating and cooling loads in this house, one small heat pump handles the house's needs.

Many mini-split systems are ductless and require just a small three-inch hole in the wall connecting the interior and exterior units. Particularly in renovations, it is much simpler and less expensive to install a ductless system than one that requires ripping out walls and ceilings to install ducts. Mini-split ductless systems are composed of three main parts—an indoor air-handling unit, an outdoor compressor/condenser unit, and a remote control that operates the system. A smartphone or computer can also control some units. Heat is transferred using refrigerant expansion and compression, in much the same way as a refrigerator works. During the colder months, a heat pump, using extremely cold refrigerant, absorbs heat from the cool outdoors and transfers it indoors. During the warmer months, the pump moves heat from the cool house to the hot outdoors. The pump moves heat rather than generates heat, so it can provide up to four times the amount of energy it consumes. One outdoor condensing unit can be used for up to eight indoor air handlers in different zones of the house, each controlled to meet the needs of certain rooms. The number of heat pumps required depends on the size of the home and how well insulated the home is.

Each of the zones has its own thermostat so only the occupied rooms can be conditioned, saving energy and money. Some units are self-correcting, so they can increase or decrease output depending on the set temperature. These systems are also small, cost less to install than traditional HVAC systems, and use a fraction of the energy, substantially reducing utility bills.

# THE MALIBU HOUSE

## MANUFACTURED*

**PHOTOGRAPHER**
Reed Fish
Upmarket Media
https://twofishdigital.com

**ARCHITECT/MANUFACTURER/GENERAL CONTRACTOR**
Dvele
(www.dvele.com)

**SIZE**
1,838 square feet

**LOCATION**
Malibu, California

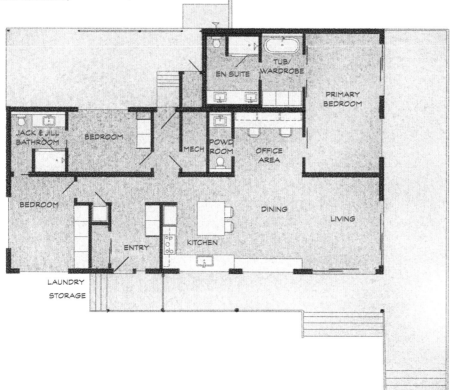

*This house is considered a manufactured house, rather than a modular, because it is built on a metal chassis, is delivered on wheels (which are not seen), and is compliant with the Department of Housing and Urban Development (HUD Code). However, this house was built in the same factory as the company's modular homes, which meet the Universal Building code and is built to the same high standards.

**E**rin Mills and her partner Barclay Neel, along with their rescue beagle-jack, Bailey, live in the Point Dume community of Malibu. The couple needed to rebuild their home at the site where their previous home was destroyed in the 2018 Woolsey Fire. The couple had closed on their new home a few weeks before the fire, which had given them just enough time to have made alterations in the house and to fully furnish it. They were set to spend their first night at the house when it burned down.

**Above:** Windows and operable glass doors surround the house, bringing in ample natural light. The large roof overhangs block some of the light in the hottest months when the sun is high in the sky.

## GREEN FEATURES

- Metal siding from recycled material
- All electric, no gas
- Induction cooktop
- Quartz countertops
- Energy recovery ventilator (ERV)

## ENERGY FEATURES

- Solar array
- Battery backup
- LED lighting
- Smart water heater
- Smart house monitoring
- Car charging station
- ENERGY STAR appliances
- Retractable sunshades

## PLANNING THEIR REPLACEMENT HOME

When Erin and Barclay were planning this new house, their goal was to rebuild using their previous floor plan with a few improvements. They considered building the house on-site but were concerned about the time and cost of that method of construction. They interviewed several builders and felt Dvele, a modular manufacturer, could best meet their modern esthetic, could build their home as energy efficient as they desired, and, with their factory construction, could build it fast and economically.

They aspired to build a modern style home, with clean lines, tall ceilings, and floor-to-ceiling windows and doors. All this glazing would minimize the barrier between the interior of the house and the outside world. The openness of the house would allow them to truly experience the joy of living along the canyon so close to the ocean. In addition to the openness, they also wanted the house to feel very cozy, comfortable, and retreatlike. Although they wanted a large amount of glazing to maximize the views, it was important that the placement of the glass still provide privacy. Dvele understood these parameters and designed their home to meet all their wishes.

**Opposite:** Sliding doors in the living room open to the porch area. Retractable sunshades can be lowered to keep out the sun when necessary.

**Right:** An open configuration was an important aspect for the owners. The light walls and high ceilings increase the perception of openness and space.

**Below:** Beautiful views can be seen from all areas of the common spaces. Natural colors and textures of the surroundings area were used in the décor to add to the warmth of the house.

## MEETING LOCAL REGULATIONS

Kurt Goodjohn, the CEO and cofounder of Dvele, said there are many regulations in this community, some in place to prevent obstructing the views of other homeowners. There were also setbacks that impacted the size of the house; this was the largest home that could be built at this location, unless it was combined with another lot. Dvele began the design process with a standard plan and added customizations that fit the homeowner's wishes and met the specifications for the configuration of the lot.

**Left:** The couple wanted the primary bedroom to have a seating area so that when they have guests, they have a place to retreat and relax on their own. The sliding glass doors further expand this space.

**Above:** The office area between the powder room and primary bedroom provides space for the couple to work at home. The large pocket door opens the space up while also being a space saver.

**Above, left:** The high window in the bathroom area brings in light while still providing privacy.

**Above, right:** The outdoor shower, just outside the en suite bathroom, is an added bonus to this house.

## BUILDING A SELF-POWERED SMART HOME

According to Goodjohn, this home is designed to be self-powered. With solar panels on the roof and a battery backup system, the house can be solar powered even in a blackout with the battery backup system (see sidebar on page 93). An energy recovery ventilator (ERV) keeps the air fresh in this tight built house when the doors are closed. The house is equipped with a clean air delivery system that provides fresh, filtered air throughout the house. An array of sensors along with an ERV ventilation system ensures that the air quality is consistently filtering out pollutants. According to the company, this system filters out over 90 percent of outdoor contaminant particles from entering the home while simultaneously exhausting air out of areas of the home that produce moisture and odors. It also circulates air when it senses carbon dioxide spikes or when the home anticipates volatile organic compound (VOC) increases from cooking.

Erin and Barclay say that although they lost their first house there, it gave them the opportunity to build their dream home. "It all worked out!" Erin stated.

**Top and bottom:** The multiple outdoor spaces vastly increase the living space of this small house.

**Left:** The house is part of the Point Dume community, located on the western tip of the Santa Monica Bay on the coast of Malibu.

# HOME BACKUP BATTERIES

Residential battery systems are becoming more popular as more and more homeowners add solar panels to their homes. According to the Solar Energy Industries Association (SEIA), there has been an annual growth of residential battery systems because of a reduction in cost for the systems, lower costs for installation, increasing electricity costs, increased power outages, and the incentives offered nationally for solar panels. SEIA says, "Homeowners and businesses are increasingly demanding solar systems that are paired with battery storage. While this pairing is still relatively new, the growth over the next five years is expected to be significant."

Batteries are charged by solar energy during the day, when the solar panels are producing more electricity than the home is consuming. This energy can be used at off-peak hours to charge an electric car and be exported to the grid to provide energy to other houses when the sun is down. During blackouts, the stored energy in the battery can be used to run appliances and other household needs. During a blackout, the average home will require 750 to 1000 watts of power per hour; a ten-kilowatt battery will last ten to twelve hours, and a twenty-kilowatt battery will last twenty to twenty-four hours. Most of the new batteries sold today are equipped with energy monitoring, metering, and smart controls that allow the homeowner to customize the information they get. Homeowners can also control the system by remote control. Today, lithium-ion batteries are the most commonly used technology. With the current technology, batteries will last from ten to fifteen years.

# PORTAGE BAY FLOATING HOME

## OFF-SITE CONSTRUCTION

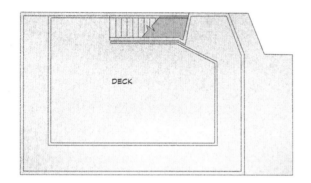

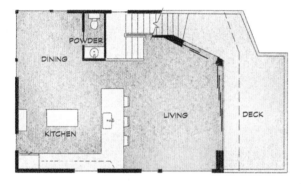

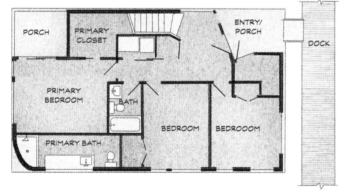

**PHOTOGRAPHER**
AJ Canaria (www.ajcan.com), unless otherwise noted

**ARCHITECT**
PBW Architects
(http://pbwarchitects.com)

**CONTRACTOR**
Building Space Construction
(www.buildingspace.ca)

**MANUFACTURER**
International Marine Floatation Systems
British Columbia
(www.floatingstructures.com)

**CONSULTANT**
Joan Rosenstock

**SIZE**
1,580 square feet

**LOCATION**
San Juan Islands, Washington

**Opposite:** This house is the second of several modern additions to this aging floating home community.

Joan Rosenstock had a passion for houseboats, after having lived in a rental at the Portage Bay community for seven years while working for the City of Seattle in urban planning. When the opportunity arose, she purchased the marina. She sold several of the moorings and decided to build two new houseboats at that location to replace some of the aging ones. This house was the second one Joan has completed at the marina.

## GREEN FEATURES

- Dual-drawer dishwasher
- Low-flow plumbing fixtures
- Quartz countertops

## ENERGY FEATURES

- Passive cooling from cross-ventilation
- Passive daylighting
- Highly insulated exterior walls
- High efficiency windows
- No air-conditioning
- Radiant floor heating
- On-demand hot water heater

## DESIGNING AND CONSTRUCTION A HOUSEBOAT

Joan was clear about the design she wanted for her new houseboat. She knew it had to have an environmentally friendly concrete mooring rather than the large log ones that were commonly used. She wanted the house to be filled with light, have lots of windows, and be strategically placed so they would still provide privacy. The staircase to the roof also had to be well placed so it would be a natural extension of the second floor living area.

Joan met one of the architects at PBW Architects when she was casually looking for advice on a porch she was building onto her current home. She was so impressed with their advice she decided to hire the firm to design the two houseboats she was about to build. After doing some research, she found the International Marine Floatation Systems in Vancouver, BC, and hired them to build her two houseboats.

**Opposite:** The glass wall in the living area opens to a spacious porch on the first floor.

**Left:** To save energy, the house is equipped with a dual-fuel stove and dishwasher drawers, so that with a smaller load only one drawer needs to be used.

**Below:** The second floor of the floating home has an open concept with large windows throughout so the residents can enjoy the beautiful water views. Radiant heating is below maple flooring throughout.

**Above, top:** One of the two secondary bedrooms has several windows and light walls making the room look more spacious.

**Above, bottom:** The primary bathroom has a large rimless shower.

## BUILDING CHALLENGES

Joan says the biggest challenge she had in building these homes was getting permits for them. After eighteen months and making several concessions, she was able to start building her home. Another challenge was meeting the City of Seattle Seismic Building Code for single family homes, which added an additional unnecessary cost to this construction, since floating homes with concrete floats won't torque or fall off their foundation as land houses might in a seismic zone.

It then took ten months to build the house at the marina in Vancouver. Joan says she had to make the trip to the marina in Canada once or twice a week to manage the construction.

Building floating homes is not very different than building ones on land, according to the contractor working on this home. However, he says, it is important that the weight of the materials be kept to a minimum wherever possible because the houses are going to be placed on a floating device. In addition, since the houses are close to other houses, the walls must meet the fire code. The contractor pointed out the importance of excellent advance planning for the utility hookups and familiarity with the docking area because these hookups can be more complicated than on land. Often other houseboats must be moved to install a new house, with hookups temporarily disconnected. In proceeding with one of these new hookups, there is a short window of time when this must be completed.

**Top:** The porch on the first floor is just one of the several outdoor spaces expanding the living area of the house.

**Bottom:** Beams in the primary bedroom add to the warmth of the room. Windows were positioned to add privacy while allowing in natural light and ventilation.

## BRINGING THE HOUSE
## TO ITS MOORING

When this house was completed in Vancouver, it was covered in a plastic wrap to make the journey to its Portage Bay mooring. Although this wrap was an added expense, the covering was necessary to prevent damage from birds and weather during the thirty-two-hour trip to Seattle.

Joan continues to have a passion for houseboats and is currently in the process of building another houseboat to replace an aging one at the marina.

**Above, top:** The house was covered with plastic wrap for the trip to Portage Bay. (Photo courtesy of Matt Tabias.)

**Above, bottom**: A tugboat brought the house from Vancouver to the moorage at Portage Bay. (Photo courtesy of Matt Tabias.)

**Right:** Windows surround the dining area providing natural daylighting and ventilation.

**Left:** Most of the house has fiber cement siding, while the lower level and entrance have vertically applied Western Cedar siding.

**Below:** The floating home is located at its moorage in Portage Bay.

# FLOATING HOMES

Floating homes are a more unusual way to live but are popular in places where there is either a history of logging or it is a flood prone area like many parts of Asia, the Netherlands, Washington State, Vancouver, British Columbia, and Sausalito, California. Floating homes are distinguished from house boats because they don't have a motor and are not built to move around. These floats are built at a marine factory on the river and then are tugged to the slip where they are hooked up to sewerage, power, water, and the internet.

The floatation device on which the house sits is a reinforced concrete shell with a core of expanded polystyrene. Each device must be carefully engineered to hold the weight of the house and keep it level even though some parts of the house will be heavier than others.

These floatation devices are unsinkable and are built with rigidity to withstand lifting and launching stresses, as well as marine environments. The floating foundations are filled 100 percent with EPS (expanded polystyrene). The company that produced the floating foundation for this house, International Marine Floatation Systems, says the device is built to outlast the structure itself. Some of the positive aspects of this concrete floating foundation is that the materials are noncombustible, maintenance free, bug and rodent proof, and use environmentally inert materials, which eliminate the use of toxic paints.

Portage Bay Floating Home was built by a company that has been building floating homes for over forty years. The exterior was built at the marine facility; it was then tugged from the Fraser River in Vancouver into the ocean, through the Washington State Locks, and finally into the Portage Bay, Seattle, community. It was completed at its mooring. All the utilities were hooked up and the house was ready for residents to move in.

# SPARC HOUSE

## PANELIZED

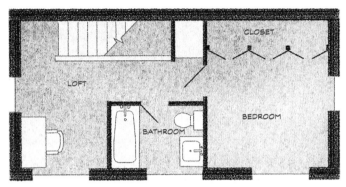

LEVEL 2

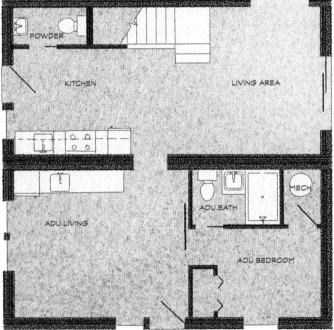

LEVEL 1

**PHOTOGRAPHER**
Kristen Taddonio (unless otherwise noted)

**ARCHITECT/GENERAL CONTRACTOR/ MANUFACTURER**
University of Colorado Boulder students and faculty
(www.cubouldersolardecathlon.com)

**GENERAL CONTRACTOR**
UC Boulder
M3 Property Services
(www.m3ps.net)

**SIMPLE HOMES (PANELIZED SYSTEM)**
(www.simplehomes.com)

**SIZE**
Primary House 1,176 square feet
Guest Suite 392 square feet

**LOCATION**
Fraser, Colorado

**Opposite:** The SPARC House was designed in dramatic black with black solar panels and standing seam roof. The side porch expands the living space of this small house.

The goal of the University of Colorado Boulder team as participants in the Solar Decathlon 2021 (see sidebar on page 111) was to create a replicable example of housing to meet the shortages and construction challenges in mountain towns across the country. They wanted to create a house that was affordable and high energy performing, with limited environmental impact and limited operating costs for owners and renters. SPARC House was their solution. They included an accessory dwelling unit that would also

## GREEN FEATURES

- Induction stove
- No gas connection
- Electric vehicle charging station
- Minimal use of foams, refrigerants, and other high global warming potential products
- Natural sheep's wool insulation
- GREENGUARD Indoor Air Quality Certified hickory flooring

## ENERGY FEATURES

- Optimal placement of high efficiency operable windows
- Ductless air source heat pumps
- Energy recovery ventilator (ERV)
- Solar array
- Building automation system
- High efficiency insulation including continuous exterior insulation and vapor-intelligent weather and air barriers
- Building automation and energy information system
- ENERGY STAR appliances
- Heat pump clothes dryer
- Car charging station
- Electric water heater (with demand response control module to maximize water heating when the solar array is powering the house)

**Top:** The lower level of the main house includes a kitchen, living room and dining room area, a powder room, and a reading nook under the stairs. Every space in the house was designed to be functional and comfortable.

**Bottom:** The appliances in the house are all ENERGY STAR rated. The flooring throughout the main living area is hickory hardwood.

bring in income and provide temporary housing for seasonal workers who support tourism in mountain towns. The team also realized that since this house was being built during the pandemic, the guest suite could provide a separate space for someone to live when they required isolation. The name of the house, SPARC, came from what the students considered the "pillars" on which the house was built: sustainability, performance, attainability, resilience, and community. The design and construction of the house, which took place from 2017 until the event in 2021, was a collaboration between more than thirty people—including sophomores to PhD students, faculty, and the eventual homeowners.

## A FORTUNATE MEETING

In a chance meeting, two CU Boulder students on the team, Hannah and Gabi, met local Fraser residents, Kristen Taddonio and Joe Smyth, who had recently bought land in the town with the hope of building a sustainable house. The couple decided to sponsor the building of the house for the Solar Decathlon competition, which they would then own. This was fortuitous for the team since they would have the opportunity to design a house for real people, in a real town. The house would be a departure from the significantly larger homes in the area and would be more sustainable and energy efficient. The couple spent approximately $400,000 to build the house which includes the land it sits on, its foundation, furnishings, and deck. This is far less than what houses in the surrounding area would cost. According to homeowner Kristen, "If this house were to be put on the market today, it would be one of the most affordable options in the region."

**Below:** The reading nook is a cozy place to relax and makes good use of the area under the staircase. A door in this area leads out to the raised porch.

## BUILDING MORE AFFORDABLE HOMES

Fraser, like many other mountain towns, is facing high housing costs and limited housing options. Local residents and seasonal workers are being pushed out of the housing market and forced to commute to work over mountain passes. Since many of the CU students and their families either live in or moved to Colorado to enjoy the access to sports and nature that these towns provide, this housing issue is close to many of their hearts. These issues sparked the students' interest in building an affordable, easily constructed house that also offered rental space.

The team visited Fraser, met with the town mayor, town council, and some locals, and learned about construction challenges in this local climate with a short build season. The team also read news reports of locals being pushed out of the area due to the high cost of housing. The team then refined their purpose to build with more specific focus on mountain towns, and Fraser specifically.

**Opposite, top:** Kristen and Joe built the dining table with a top made of acacia, a fast-growing sustainable wood, and the legs are made of steel. It's longer and narrower than a standard table as they wanted to be able to seat eight people in a shape that wouldn't feel too large for the space.

**Opposite, bottom:** A comfortable seating area is just above the stairs in the main house.

**Above:** The barn door leads from the living/kitchen area of the guest suite to the bedroom and bathroom areas. The ceiling is pine beetle kill pine to add coziness to this small area, and the flooring is hickory hardwood.

## CONSTRUCTION ISSUES

About a year before the event, the team discovered that the house they had initially designed was not going to fit on the lot. They determined that building the house with a panelized system would allow them to build the house with the space they needed on two floors. The team partnered with Simple Homes, a panelization company out of Denver, where they learned to build the panels in their warehouse. The project tested a partially closed assembly in which sheep's wool insulation and vapor-intelligent wraps were applied in the warehouse with the intent of saving on-site construction time and construction materials exposure to the elements.

Simple Homes transported the fifteen large panels to Fraser where the house structure was erected in just two days. The team recognized that using such a prefab system would help with the labor shortage in the area and would also aid in the short building season in these mountain areas. Prefab factories can function twelve months a year even in challenging weather conditions.

With the onset of the pandemic, many students moved back to their homes far from Fraser, and completing construction became a challenge, along with the safety issues around the virus. This situation required some hands-on help by the homeowners, along with regular drives to the house by the students who lived in town and the students who made regular drives from Boulder, a two-hour drive away.

With all the challenges faced by the students, the CU Boulder team won the event in 2021. Kristen and Joe are now delighted homeowners of the SPARC house.

**Top:** The homeowners charge their car with the energy they capture with the solar panels.

**Bottom:** The panels arrived in Fraser from the Simple Homes factory on a flatbed truck. (Photo courtesy of Jennifer Scheib.)

# SOLAR DECATHLON

Since the Solar Decathlon began in 2002, thousands of students from colleges around the world have competed to design and construct high-performance, low carbon homes powered by renewables. The Solar Decathlon is an educational program of the US Department of Energy (DOE) and is organized by the National Renewable Energy Laboratory (NREL). Since the initial Solar Decathlon in the US, the program has expanded internationally with events in Africa, China, Europe, India, Latin America and the Caribbean, and the Middle East. Due to the pandemic, the event took place virtually for the first time in 2021. Whereas past events have generally occurred at a central location—such as the National Mall in Washington, DC—future Solar Decathlon houses will be competed and displayed in the community where they are constructed. This will give local residents the opportunity to visit the houses and participate in tours by student teams.

It is difficult not to be inspired by the innovative, beautiful, energy efficient houses at the event, and by the bright students who give tours of their houses. They have impressive knowledge of the mechanics of their houses and explain all the systems and considerations behind the design decisions to visitors. The Solar Decathlon is a great educational opportunity for the public to experience the variety of prefabricated building methods, systems, materials, and techniques that can be used to build more sustainable, healthy, and efficient homes.

In each Solar Decathlon competition student teams compete in ten contests. The 2021 contests were Energy Performance, Engineering, Financial Feasibility and Affordability, Resilience, Architecture, Operations (hot water, appliances, etc.), Market Potential, Comfort and Environmental Quality, Innovation, and Presentation. The decathlon categories can change each cycle; for the 2023 competition, an Embodied Environmental Impact contest has been added to encourage teams to consider and reduce the life-cycle resource use of their houses.

According to Holly Carr, the director of the Solar Decathlon at the US Department of Energy, "We are beginning the third decade of the Solar Decathlon, and zero-energy homes are becoming more accessible and cost effective. Students participating in the competition continue to gain unparalleled experience that prepares them to be leaders in the transition to a clean energy economy."

# BOXABL CASITA

## STRUCTURAL INSULATED PANELS (SIPS)/MODULAR

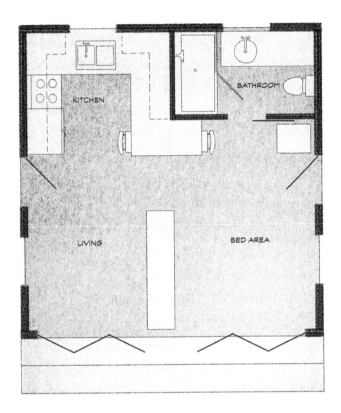

**PHOTOGRAPHER**
Charles Henry Garland (unless otherwise noted)
(www.theprogenyphoto.com)

**DESIGNERS**
Paolo Tiramani, Galiano Tiramani, Kyle Denman

**MANUFACTURER**
Boxabl
(www.boxabl.com)

**SIZE**
375 square feet

**LOCATION**
North Las Vegas, Nevada

**Opposite:** The model of the Casita sits on the lot next to the factory in Las Vegas, Nevada.

Boxabl, the company that produces the Casita, was the brain-child of Paolo Tiramani, the CEO of the company. He received degrees in industrial design and mechanical engineering from Central School London and in more recent years has studied the best methods of home construction. In 2017 he started Boxabl with his business partner and son Galiano with the goal of mass-producing houses in a factory—fast, strong, of high quality, and inexpensively. He not only studied the technology of building houses to meet his goals, but also the machines to build the houses similar to the way automobiles are now built.

After several years of product development, the first production model was presented in 2020 at the International Builders Show in Las Vegas. The company received an initial order from the US Army to build 156 units, which are the first houses the company shipped. Afterward they began production on the Casitas for residential

## GREEN FEATURES
- LED lights
- Low carbon emissions

## ENERGY FEATURES
- Structural insulated panels (SIPs)
- Mini-split heat pump
- High efficiency appliances
- High efficiency windows

---

**Above:** The model in Las Vegas is open on one side to view the entire interior.

**Opposite, top:** Although the floor plan is small, the kitchen, and sleeping and living areas are separated to provide a more expansive feel.

**Opposite, bottom:** The sliding barn door allows light to enter the bathroom and minimizes space required for the opening.

customers. The goal of the company is to bring assembly-line efficiency to the prefabricated housing industry, a transition Tiramani believes is long overdue.

The Casitas are built to meet modular code, which means they will conform to most state building codes. The homes are inspected in the factory, reducing the need for local inspections when the house is set, and the plans are preapproved by the states in which they will be located.

## LITTLE REQUIREMENTS NEEDED ON THE INTERIOR

The first edition Casitas are shipped with complete bathrooms and kitchens (with refrigerator, stove, microwave, and dishwasher), washer/dryer, wide plank composite wood flooring (see sidebar on page 119), cabinetry, air-conditioning, a backlit mirror in the bathroom, breakfast bar, and a sliding glass barn door. Homeowners just need to add the furnishings on the interior. According to Tiramani, future models will be multibox units and will include preinstalled full staircases, fireplaces, and powder rooms.

## BUILT WITH STRUCTURAL INSULATED PANELS (SIPS)

The design concept was to build a structure that could withstand hurricanes and other harsh weather conditions. The Casitas are clad with noncombustible materials. Although nothing can withstand raging fires like those that have been the norm in the West, the exterior will withstand flying embers. The company produces their own structural insulated panels (SIPs), fusing together galvanized steel for the outer layers, MGO (magnesium oxide) for the interior layer, and EPS (expanded polystyrene) in the center. The MGO is one of the components of Portland Cement and is used in place of drywall because it is more stable and fireproof. No commonly used lumber or drywall is used in the construction. The building materials are less likely to become moldy if damaged by water.

**Top:** All of the appliances and cabinetry are included in the Casita when it is shipped.

**Bottom:** The counter on the wall provides a casual eating space.

## ON-SITE WORK REQUIRED

Prior to the house being shipped, the homeowner employs a contractor to build a foundation and once the house arrives at the site, connections must be made for utility hookups. Utilities easily plug in on-site at the exterior corner of the Casita. If the homeowner prefers a pitched roof, the company will provide the plans, but it will be the owner's responsibility to add the new roof and a recommended gutter system.

The house is built with chases in the walls with all the plumbing, electric, and HVAC preinstalled, which will be plugged in on-site. Additional costs include obtaining permits, as well as land-scaping. Casitas can be personalized with any style the homeowner wants on the exterior. According to Tiramani, the Casita is "architecturally neutral"; homeowners can personalize it to any style they like.

**Top:** The bathroom includes a self-lit mirror and a high set window to allow in light and fresh air while also providing privacy.

**Bottom:** Windows and sliding doors bring ample natural light and ventilation into the structure.

**Left:** The current Boxabl factory is 305,000 square feet, with a 4 million-square-foot factory in the planning. (Photo courtesy of David Thompson.)

**Right:** The Casita structure takes about an hour to unfold. This is the folded Casita. (Photo courtesy of Boxabl.)

## OVERCOMING SHIPPING ISSUES

Because the houses are only eight and a half feet high, twenty feet long, and twenty feet wide, they can be transported easily by truck or shipped anywhere in the world. According to the company, the house is folded and can be reassembled in an hour. When the house is unfolded, the ceiling has a nine-foot six-inch interior ceiling height.

The best thing about the current Casita is the price at $69,000. Tiramani's vision is to sell these Casitas in the future directly through big box stores and major on-line sellers. A "Boxabl University" is in the works to train workers to connect and complete all aspects of the units. Tiramani says his feeling about this business from the start was that "something very special is happening." At this writing, Boxabl has orders for more than 130,000 units and is in the process of building a massive new factory. The future looks very bright for this company.

# COMPOSITE WOOD FLOORING

Composite wood, also known as engineered wood, is composed of multiple layers of crisscrossed plywood layers of wood fused together with glue, heat, and high pressure. It has a center core and a harder top layer to resist damage. Composite wood is used for its durability, moisture resistance, and ease of installation. The flooring panels can be glued, nailed, or stapled onto the floor or floated with snap-together tongue-and-groove edges for easy installation.

Composite flooring is often indistinguishable from a solid wood floor. It does not absorb water and can be used with radiant heating. However, it is more environmentally friendly than solid wood flooring because it uses wood cut from solid planks from fast-growing trees and is particularly more eco-friendly when it uses non-formaldehyde-based adhesives and urethane-based finishes, which can pollute the air indoors. Thicker composite wood flooring is more durable because the top layer can be refinished once or twice when damaged, while those with thinner top layers will have to be replaced. Bamboo is often used for composite flooring since the wood is not thick enough for wide planks, and it is very eco-friendly because bamboo is a very fast-growing "grass."

Composite flooring is a desirable option because it is prefinished, easier to install than solid wood, will not crack, cup, split, and expand with moisture, and is durable and eco-friendly.

# VINEYARD VISTA

## MODULAR

**PHOTOGRAPHER**
Gregory D. Specht
(https://gregorydeanphotography.com)

**ARCHITECT**
Jim Russell
ideabox LLC
(www.ideabox.us)

**GENERAL CONTRACTOR**
Terry Hall
Square Deal Construction Company
(https://squaredeal.construction)

**MANUFACTURER**
Stratford Building Corporation
(https://stratfordbuild.com)

**SIZE**
1,473 square feet

**LOCATION**
Newberg, Oregon

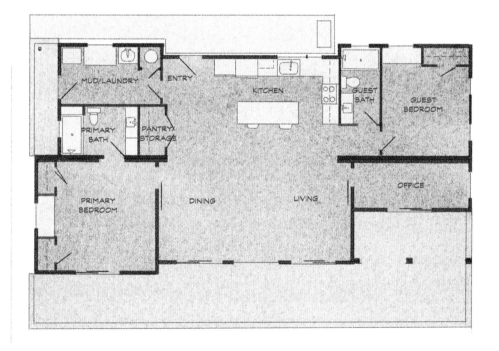

Robert Newton and John Brackett lived in San Francisco and then later in a condo in the bustling Pearl District of Portland until they decided they wanted a change from an urban environment to a more tranquil setting. After searching for a few months, they found an ideal two-and-a-half-acre lot in Newburg, Oregon.

**Above:** The house was designed with two very low maintenance sidings—fiber cement and metal. Large overhangs on the house deflect some of the hot sun in the warmer months.

## GREEN FEATURES

- Recycled metal roofing and siding
- Fiber cement siding
- No VOC paints
- Whole house exhaust fan

## ENERGY FEATURES

- High efficiency windows and doors
- LED lighting
- Heat pump water heating
- Ductless heat pumps and zonal heating
- Large overhangs

**Above:** The clerestory windows bring added light and ventilation into the common areas. The couple incorporated the furniture they had from their Portland condo, buying only a new dining room table and a bed for the additional bedroom they gained.

## BUILDING PREFAB

Robert and John had extensive experience with major remodels in San Francisco which led them to the decision that they didn't want to endure the stress of a site-built home. They also thought prefab construction would be a lower cost alternative to site building, where costs rise when last-minute decisions lead to changes in the design or materials or both. They read about modular construction and, after searching online, found ideabox: a modular company with the modern aesthetic they sought, which was also in close proximity to their lot. The couple met with the ideabox team and immediately knew the designers understood the look and feel they hoped to achieve for their new home.

Robert and John say it was very exciting to see one of the company's model houses and experience the finishes and workmanship. The ideabox team worked closely with them, walking them through the whole process from design to placement on the property. Going from a design on paper to a real house delivered to their site was "a bit surreal," they say. With the house being built in a factory, they were able to have some distance from the day-to-day construction as well as avoid costly change orders. The house arrived at the site in October 2019 and they were able to move in one month later as their general contractor was very efficient in completing the on-site work.

**Right:** The kitchen was kept light and airy with white cabinets and appliances and light wood flooring.

**Below:** The open concept, a large amount of glazing, and high ceilings make this house appear bigger than it is. Although the footprint by square footage is smaller than any of the couple's other homes, the open concept makes it feel large.

## ENERGY EFFICIENCY AS A PRIORITY

Since the winters could be cold and the summers hot in this area, ensuring the house was well insulated and built with energy efficient materials was very important. They wanted all the windows to be high efficiency and the home to have a white membrane roof, which would reflect some of the summer heat. The house was positioned on the lot for optimal solar orientation, facing south to capture the sun in the winter, and built with large overhangs to block the sun during summer. Two ductless mini-split heat pumps were installed for heating and cooling, with an option for a third if required. The main living space is well served by one of the units and the second unit is in the main bedroom. They haven't had to install the third unit in the second bedroom since the room stays cool in the summer. An installed electric heater in the second bedroom provides heat when needed in the winter.

**Right:** The main bedroom and the guest room are on opposite sides of the house.

## MAXIMIZING SPACE

One of the ways they maximized space in the house was with barn doors (see sidebar on page 129). Robert and John first used them years ago in a bathroom as a design feature and to save space. When they were designing the new house, they felt barn doors would also be a good feature in this small space. They also opted for an open floor plan and lots of glazing. The interior is kept light with light-colored wood flooring, light walls, and a white kitchen. The light walls are a great backdrop for the couple's family heirloom pictures and paintings, which have traveled with them to all their homes.

**Below:** A special heirloom desk was the inspiration for the home office design.

**Top:** The guest room on the other side of the house from the main bedroom offers both space and privacy for visitors.

**Bottom:** The front porch is a wonderful place to enjoy the beautiful natural vista.

# FIBER CEMENT SIDING

Fiber cement siding is an increasingly popular exterior cladding material. Made of sand, cement, and cellulose fibers, it comes primed, stained, painted, or as raw siding in lap siding, panels, and shingles. It is also available smooth or textured with a look of wood, stucco, stone, or brick. The siding is more durable and less expensive than wood and works particularly well in hot, humid climates where regular wood siding is prone to rot and fungus.

Because it doesn't have knots and other inconsistencies of wood, fiber cement siding is more durable and holds paint better, which reduces maintenance costs. In addition to low maintenance, the siding resists moisture, warping, shrinking, cracking, fading, termites and other insect damage, fire, and impact damage. The James Hardie siding used on this house has a thirty-year limited warranty.

**Below:** A large deck in the front of the house adds to the living space.

# BARN DOORS

Barn doors are known not only for their functionality but also serve as decorative design elements. They are space savers, functioning as basic doors, flush with the wall, making them perfect for use in rooms where there is no space for doors to swing in and out. Barn doors can be used to close off rooms, hide television sets, or divide a room. They can also be closet doors or exterior doors. There are a multitude of designs available to fit any type of decor from rustic to modern. Another advantage is that barn doors don't distract from a seamless view of the wall, because there is no extending hardware or angles of a traditional door. Standard doors often encroach on living space instead of being just part of the wall.

Barn doors can be bought as antiques, salvaged from old barns or houses, built by handy do-it-yourselfers, or purchased new. Sometimes authentic old barn doors are restored or old doors from other houses are repurposed as barn doors. These can be used in pairs or individually and can be hung from a bar with rollers or have coasters at the top or a rail at the bottom.

# TROPICAL PANORAMA

## INSULATED CONCRETE FORMS (ICFS) WALLS

**PHOTOGRAPHER**
Steve Simonsen

**ARCHITECTS**
Zach Gasper
Mark Turner
GreenSpur
(www.greenspur.net)

**GENERAL CONTRACTOR**
Cross Island Builders
(www.crossisland.com)

**MANUFACTURER**
Quad-Lock
(www.quadlock.com)

**SIZE**
1,950 square feet

**LOCATION**
St. John, United States Virgin Islands

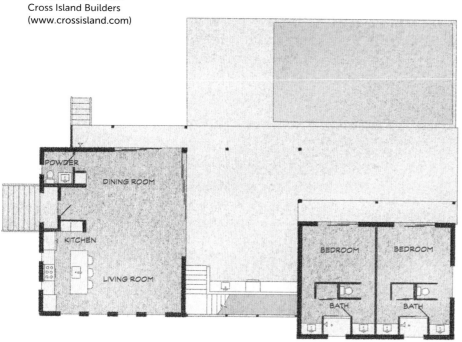

The story of this villa is about natural destruction and rebuilding under the threat of future disasters as well as using sustainable methods while respecting the natural landscape of the land.

The Campbell family bought this villa in 2015. They loved the location perched above Cruz Bay, with its beautiful views from the large windows, and the swimming pool, which was the first private pool on the island of St. John. They enjoyed family time there until it was destroyed by two back-to-back category 5 hurricanes, Irma and Maria, in 2017. All that was left at the site was the foundation and the cistern, which collected water. As devastating as the hurricanes were, it gave the family the opportunity to rebuild the house with more modern construction that would weather future storms.

**Below:** The new house is perched above Cruz Bay with beautiful views of the mountains and water below.

## GREEN FEATURES

- Cistern water collection
- Native landscaping
- No natural gas in the house
- Plumbing monitoring system
- Electric monitoring system
- No ducts (with split-air AC system)

## ENERGY FEATURES

- Large overhangs
- Ceiling fans
- Louvered shutters
- Insulated roof
- Precast insulated foundation
- High efficiency windows
- Insulated concrete form (ICF) walls
- Window placement (based on breeze and sun studies)

To capture the beautiful views and sunsets, the owners worked with architects Zach Gasper and Mark Turner of GreenSpur to use the existing footprint to create a new home. They wanted to create a home with seamless indoor-outdoor spaces to capture the sea view from all rooms and to allow air to flow throughout all the living spaces.

**Above, top:** The interior of the house is all open concept with large sliding doors connecting the interior with the exterior living areas of the house. Fans in the inside and outdoor living space reduce the need for air-conditioning.

**Above, bottom:** The inside dining area is barely separated from the outside with ninety degrees of glazing.

**Opposite:** With the pool lit up in the evening, the house provides a wonderful place to entertain both night and day.

## A CHALLENGING REBUILD

With no electricity, no physical permit office, limitations on getting building materials to the island, and a limited work force, it was a challenge to rebuild the house after the hurricanes. Since owner David Campbell had been working in construction as an engineer, builder, and developer, he was used to solving difficult construction issues and was undeterred from rebuilding his home. Through his business, he had worked with architects Zack Gasper and Mark Turner in the past on other projects and asked them to design their new home to replace the one they lost. He told Gasper and Turner that his priority was to prevent the new house from ever getting destroyed by another hurricane.

The architects struggled with what was left to build upon structurally, complicated by the non-existence of any records showing the original 1960s engineering of the house. Through several site visits, lots of photographs, and a creative structural engineer, the team was able to work through structural issues and use some modern and sustainable techniques like insulated concrete form (ICF) walls (see sidebar on page 137), and laminated structural beams.

Concrete was chosen for the new house because of its durability against harsh weather conditions. ICF, a prefab construction method, was selected because of the speed of construction, the energy efficiency of the walls, and the ability of these walls to withstand high force winds. This was also a good choice because construction crews are used to working with concrete on the island. The owners decided to make some minor changes in the new design by moving the location of the pool and the location of the kitchen, otherwise, the footprint was similar to the original home.

**Opposite, top:** There is an entire living area on the outer patio including a living room setup, dining area, and full kitchen.

**Opposite, bottom:** The bedrooms all have access to the exterior and the beautiful views. Mini-split heat pumps are located in all of the rooms.

**Above:** The appliances are all run on electricity, avoiding the need for natural gas.

## MINIMIZING THE ENERGY NEEDS

The design team was able to take advantage of modern 3D design software that allowed them to assess the sun's impact on the space and create a design using passive solar strategies to minimize energy requirements and maximize performance throughout the year. Since energy is expensive in the Virgin Islands, the design of the house had to incorporate factors such as the direction of the breezes, the impact of light, and the R-value* of windows and walls. The old house had no air-conditioning, which was added in the new construction. But the ICF walls limit the need for air-conditioning through its thermal mass, keeping the cost of energy down. The home fully meets code and is now rated to withstand over 200-mile-an-hour winds.

---

*R-value is the measure of thermal resistance to heat flow through a given insulating material. The higher the R-value of a material, the greater the insulating effectiveness.

## BUILDING A RESILIENT, EFFICIENT HOME

When building in these remote islands, sustainability is born out of necessity. Water comes almost exclusively from rain collected from rooftops and stored in giant cisterns. Landscape material and features come from the landscape itself since it is not cost effective to ship rocks and other landscaping materials to the islands. Like the Campbells, other owners on the island are now building stronger homes due to the more aggressive storms the area is susceptible to. Because of ICF infiltrated with lots of rebar, hurricane-proof windows, and thoughtful engineering, this home should be around a long time. Window placement, louvered shutters, and large shaded roof lines keep the energy cost to a minimum and also provide nice shade for the space to be fully enjoyed.

**Top:** The pool, now on the same level as the main living area, was relocated so the beautiful views of the ocean could be seen.

**Bottom:** The outdoor shower at the rear of the house is an open but private place to wash up after a day at the beach or the pool.

# INSULATED CONCRETE FORM (ICF) WALLS AND FOUNDATIONS

Concrete has always been a popular building material for the Caribbean region, and currently Insulating concrete forms (ICFs) are becoming more popular because of their high level of energy efficiency. ICFs consist of two foam panels, usually made from high density expanded polystyrene (EPS), that are connected with plastic ties to create a variable width concrete formwork, ranging from four to twelve inches or more, depending on the engineering needs of the building design.

The forms are stacked to the specifications of the plans with reinforcing steel added at every level. Window and door openings are cut into the foam and reinforced with temporary wooden formwork. Architectural features like arched windows are easily created with the lightweight and easy-to-cut foam panels.

Concrete is then placed in the wall cavity and the ICF panels are left in place to provide a double layer of permanent, water-resistant insulation across the entire interior and exterior of the building. This method of continuous insulation interrupts the transmission of heat through the building envelope (called "thermal bridging"). With a steel-reinforced concrete core, the house is protected against hurricanes, fire, and earthquakes, and noise infiltration is reduced. The high-mass concrete walls are a natural barrier against heat gain within the building as temperatures swing throughout the day, lessening the need for air-conditioning.

Because the forms are light in weight, they are easy to ship and most can be set in place without the use of lifting devices. ICF is an environmentally friendly system since the concrete often contains a high content of recycled fly ash, a residue produced during the combustion of coal at coal-fired electrical plants. The rebar is made from 80 percent recycled steel. In some areas, houses built with ICF qualify for insurance discounts. These walls can be used for above-ground walls as well as foundations.

The ICF forms used for this house were produced by Quad-Lock Building Systems in Atlanta, Georgia. According to Quad-Lock, "High continuous insulation combined with low air infiltration and the thermal mass of concrete provides at least 57 percent better R-value than typical wood or steel frame walls."

# CONEXUS HOUSE

## MODULAR

**PHOTOGRAPHER**
Chris Coe
(www.Chriscoephoto.com)

**ARCHITECT**
DXA studio
(www.dxastudio.com)

**DEVELOPER/OWNER**
Liv-Connected
(www.liv-connected.com)

**MANUFACTURER**
ATOMIC Homes
(www.atomicdesign.tv)

**SIZE**
500 square feet

**LOCATION**
Elizabethtown, Pennsylvania

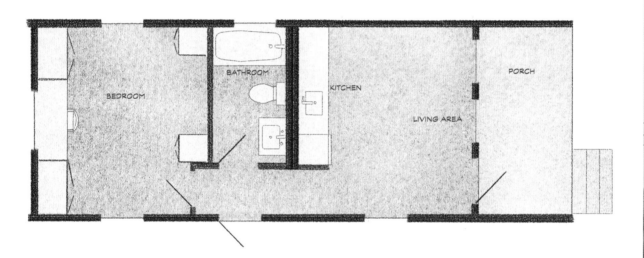

The name Conexus comes from the Latin word for "connected" or "linked," and was selected as the name of the homes built by Liv-Connected because the components are literally connected. This house is the model for future homes by Liv-Connected that will be factory-built, affordable, energy efficient, sustainable, and an innovative, new type of housing.

## GREEN FEATURES

- No formaldehyde
- Low VOC materials and finishes
- Metal roofing and siding with recycled content

## ENERGY FEATURES

- LED lights
- High efficiency windows and glazed doors
- Mini-split system
- ENERGY STAR appliances

**Above and opposite, left:** The walls and ceiling are clad in finished birch plywood.

**Opposite, right:** There is an open flow through the house from the front to the rear.

## DESIGN AND DEVELOPMENT OF THE CONEXUS

Architects Jordon Rogove and Wayne Norbeck, founding partners at DXA studio and the owners of Liv-Connected, along with Dr. Herb Rogove, a physician and a pioneer in telemedicine, and Joe Wheeler, a professor at Virginia Tech School of Architecture and Design, worked to develop this new concept. Wheeler has been involved with modular construction for many years and has been a consultant on several entry houses at Solar Decathlon events (see sidebar on page 111). He was instrumental in developing the unique design for these houses. This Conexus model was designed both for homeowners looking for an affordable, efficient home as well as in response to the ongoing struggles of both temporary and permanent disaster relief housing.

## A NEW FORM OF MODULAR CONSTRUCTION

The company calls this new prefab system Component Linked Construction (CLiC System), which is their method of building individual components and links of the house in the factory so they can more easily be transported and assembled on-site. The house is made up of five basic components—two end walls, a kitchen, bathroom, and bedroom—that are then fit together and filled in by additional links and roof components. Additional rooms can be added onto the structure as the need arises. The CLiC system also allows the homes to be disassembled and moved, especially for disaster relief applications where they might be reused.

These segments are easier to ship than traditional modular components. The linked pieces can fold down and be shipped in larger component pieces, so a one-bedroom house is able to fit on a single flatbed truck. Instead of the limitation on widths required for transporting typical modules, these can be wider while being shipped on a standard width trailer since they can fit on a truck lengthwise. This new method also eliminates the need for wide loads and escort trucks to deliver the units.

In lieu of cranes used to lift typical modulars, a telehandler (a type of forklift) can move these sections in a matter of hours. A crane may be needed for a two-story layout, or if it's needed to navigate unique site conditions. It takes approximately four to six hours to set a house, with minimal finishing work required, which includes the final trimming and sealing of the envelope.

**Below:** The kitchen countertops and backsplash are solid surface. The flooring is waterproof vinyl plank.

## BUILDING WITH EFFICIENCY

The company has been diligent in streamlining the fabrication process for maximum efficiency, practically eliminating construction waste from the building process. A well-sealed envelope has also been a priority. The house is fitted with high performance doors, windows, and insulation. A high-efficiency electric split system is used for heating and cooling, and an abundance of windows and glass-filled doors provide natural light, reducing the demand for artificial lighting. This standard unit model is solar ready and uses LED lighting, low VOC materials and finishes, and ENERGY STAR appliances.

**Top:** Every room in the house has windows to expand the feel of the living space as well as provide natural ventilation and daylighting. Even the doors have glass panels to allow in more light.

**Bottom:** Bathroom walls are waterproof vinyl tile and the flooring is waterproof vinyl plank. The countertop is solid surface.

**Above:** The porch decking is whitewashed composite wood and the vertical cladding is natural cedar that will patina over time.

## FUTURE OFFERINGS

Beyond the base Conexus model, the company will offer an upgraded Green Package that includes a solar array with battery storage, additional insulation, and an energy recovery ventilator (ERV) unit for fresh air exchange.

The company also plans to offer a health package as an upgrade. This will include full house fall detection, mechanisms to raise and lower cabinets for accessibility, direct physician access, "hospital at home" equipment including vital sign and stroke symptom detection, and a digital hub for all healthcare monitoring devices that ties into a smart vanity mirror.

The Conexus home starts at $150,000, which does not include the cost of the land, site work, connection of utilities, and limited finish work. The house can be expanded later by adding a bedroom or extending the living room, costs which would run between $30,000 and $40,000. To minimize costly customization, the company offers several exterior finish and interior finish options and several models customers can select from, as they would when purchasing a car.

The owners say, "The ultimate goal is to provide practical and uplifting solutions to the current housing crisis." They aim to make buying a home like purchasing a car: The customer can pick a model and layout, choose a finish, and place an order. They will also offer assistance with site selection, local approvals, and mortgages through a partnership they have with Rocket Mortgage.

# COMPOSITE DECKING

Composite decking is becoming more and more popular for several reasons. Older wood decking used to cause splinters that wreaked havoc on bare feet and would easily rot and decay from being exposed to the elements. And now there is also a shortage of lumber, particularly redwood and cedar—the types of wood naturally resistant to pests and decay.

Composite decking in most cases is indistinguishable from wood, is more durable, is weather resistant, and won't splinter. It is also low maintenance and does not require the chemical finishes required to maintain wood. Many companies offer twenty-five- to fifty-year warranties on their composite products.

Composite decking is made of wood fibers and plastic, much of which is made up of recycled materials. The wood fibers bond with the plastic—polypropylene or polyethylene—creating a strong bond. The decking is available in a variety of textures and colors with options such as crosscuts, wire-brushing, and low-gloss finishes. These mimic a variety of wood species such as redwood and white oak. Regional codes now require all decking material to be slip resistant, which was once an issue with composite decking.

The decking used on this house was produced by TimberTech, which advertises that 100 percent of the wood fibers they source are reclaimed and certified sustainable.

# THE PINK HOUSE

## KIT HOUSE

**PHOTOGRAPHER**
Luis Ayala/Ayala Vargas Architectural
Photography
Catama Builders, Ltd.

**ARCHITECT**
Brett Zamore Design
(www.brettzamoredesign.com)

**GENERAL CONTRACTOR**
Camilo Parra
Catama Builders, Ltd.

**SIZE**
1,800 square feet

**LOCATION**
Houston, Texas

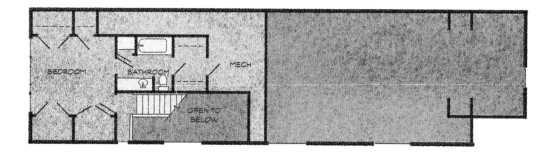

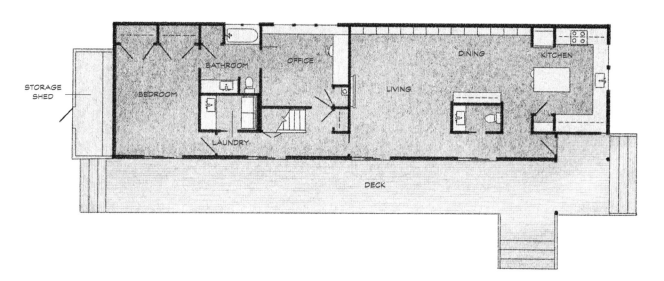

**Opposite:** The high-pitched roof has standing seam Galvalume metal. The siding is fiber cement, and the exterior doors and windows are made of wood with metal cladding and argon-gas insulated glazing. The entry door is custom made.

After having lived in a 600-square-foot apartment for thirty-two years, this couple, he an architect and she a physician, decided to upsize into a house. They purchased a decaying 1936 steel frame and stucco house they initially planned to renovate, but after reviewing the long-term building deterioration, decided it would not be financially or time prudent to do so.

## GREEN FEATURES

- Recycled materials
- Low-flow water fixtures
- Standing seam roof with recycled content
- Fiber cement board
- High SEER (seasonal energy efficiency rating) rated mechanicals
- No slab (wood foundation on drilled piers)

## ENERGY FEATURES

- Tankless water heater
- Passive ventilation and lighting
- ENERGY STAR appliances
- Extra Insulation

The homeowners opted to build a new residence. The owner and Brett Zamore, the architect for the project, were academic and professional associates. After seeing several of Zamore's kit house plans on the architect's website and in person, the owners decided to purchase one of his kit plans. They then worked with Zamore to modify and personalize the plans to meet their needs. The couple made several changes to the original design, adding more windows in the front of the house, transoms over the doors, and extra storage.

**Above:** The four double-glass doors leading out to the porch provide generous natural ventilation and daylight. The couple obtained permission to salvage the "Leaping Dancer" stainless steel artwork by architect Natalye Appel when Downtown's Jones Plaza initiated new construction as the Lynn Wyatt Square for the Performing Arts in the Theater District.

**Below, left:** The owners specified Sherwin-Williams Charming Pink as their exterior paint color, which recalls for them their former Houston neighborhood where they had admired two pink houses, both with white trim and dark green shutters. The original 1936 house on the property was also a light pink color. The siding is fiber cement.

**Below, right:** This 20-by 25-foot, high sloped gable wall serves as the focal point of the house, separating the public and private areas. The wall paint is Yves Klein International Blue. Here the sunlight beams through a transom window and reflects off the stainless-steel gas fireplace creating a beautiful daytime effect.

**Left:** The kitchen sculpture, "Pick Up Sticks" by Kelly O'Brien and Patrick Renner, hovers above the kitchen island and is prominently visible from the street—private art for public viewing. It was sculpted of salvaged steel rafter framing from the 1936 duplex that originally occupied the site. This sculpture was commissioned as a 2019 birthday gift and installed during construction.

**Below:** Flanking the north-facing windows above the kitchen's white oak cabinetry is a custom wallpaper—the "E3 Bindu" by Graciella Socorro (artist) and Carlos Ocando (photographer). The display is also partially visible from the street.

**Opposite:** The first floor's open plan concept includes the kitchen, dining area, and sitting area. At the opening to the kitchen/dining area is the art piece "All Paint Sales Final" by Patrick Renner, 2020. It consists of salvaged paint can lids from the artist's various projects, nailed to unpainted canvas over a plywood frame. Flooring throughout the house is 2¼-inch white oak strips.

## ALTERING THE PLANS

When the couple met with Zamore, they told him it was important to work around the two beautiful large oak trees on the property, which were to be the living focus of their plan's design. Since they opted not to build a garage, it was necessary to have a designated storage space (the attached shed at the south end of the main house), plus extensive storage throughout the house. They also requested to have bookshelves for their library collection and areas to display their growing art collection. Because the house is next to a fiberoptic communications facility, which emits continuous white noise, they needed additional insulation on the west side of the house to block out the noise and reduce solar heat gain. An STC-rated*, staggered, double-stud wall framing assembly, in addition to the owner's library of approximately 4,000 books, buffers the sound.

---

*Sound transmission class (STC) is a rating of sound isolation of a building wall assembly.

**Left:** With the configuration of this house like a shotgun design, one can see from the entrance to the rear of the house.

**Right:** This all-white bathroom is off the primary bedroom. The colorful "Roses & Hearts on a Blue Sky" in the bedroom is a nice contrast.

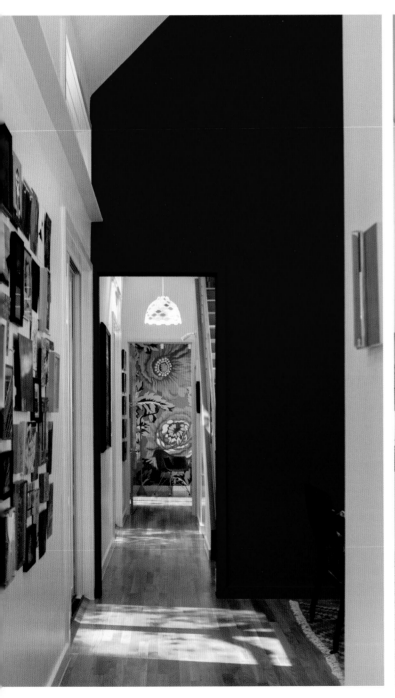

**Above:** Serving as the 17-by-9-foot headboard in the primary bedroom is the "Roses & Hearts on a Blue Sky" (by Nataliya Scheib) on the bedroom wall creates an interesting contrast to the white bathroom. It was originally installed in the Downtown District's Art Blocks program. Here it serves as the shotgun plan's end point. The owners consider this artwork "a new call for flower power's peace in turbulent times."

## DESIGN CONSIDERATIONS

The couple liked the idea of a shotgun-style house, where one can see from the front door all the way to the back of the house. Generally, there is an opening at the rear of the house for views and to allow air to flow through, but the couple decided to put their primary bedroom at the rear, where there was no opportunity or need for a back door. However, the house was designed with passive ventilation and lighting with four large sliding glass doors that run the length of the house, opening to most of the rooms and the east side yard. Since the house is in flood-prone Houston, it is pier-raised thirty inches above grade for flood protection, further allowing crawlspace airflow and maximizing on-site stormwater detention and absorption beneath the structure.

The northern front half of the house is a vaulted double-height section containing the street-facing kitchen and library-lined dining and living areas. The southern back half houses the first-floor private areas of the owners' bedroom and bathroom, laundry, and home office, plus a second-floor retreat.

**Above:** The upstairs retreat has a couch that folds out as a bed. The rug was reclaimed by the owner from a Himalayan rug company that used these swatches to display the available colors for custom rug making.

## EXTENDED CONSTRUCTION TIME

The couple purchased the property in 2001 but didn't begin the construction until August 2019. The exterior of the house was framed with windows and doors and siding completed; the interior work was initiated when the COVID-19 lockdown went into effect. The general contractor required the various trades to work one crew at a time, delaying the house's completion by two months. However, the delayed work schedule was beneficial since it allowed more time to focus on construction details and the trades were able to work more efficiently, without interference from other workers. The owners moved into their new house in late October 2020, only two months later than originally scheduled.

**Left:** The stairs leading up to the second-floor retreat are flanked by the owners' university diplomas. The hall pendant is "LC Shutters" by Louise Campbell for Louis Poulsen.

**Right:** Above the stairway and under the roof's rafter framing is "Lost Oak Branch" by Sarah Welch with James Beard and Jacob Spacek. It was commissioned as a 2021 present for the owner's birthday and installed on Arbor Day 2022. The homeowners consider it in reverence to a tree branch necessarily de-limbed for the construction of the neighbor's residence.

**Above:** The owner refers to this home office as her snuggery. The "Splugen Brau" pendant light is by Achille and Pier Giacomo Castiglioni; the painting is a reproduction of Gustav Klimt's "Apple Tree."

The owners say, "We adore our little pink house; it works perfectly for us. We cannot begin to fully convey our gratitude to the full team who made real our dream. Our pink house has served us so well throughout the pandemic, and we embrace our remaining lifetime together in this amazing house."

# TANKLESS WATER HEATERS

A typical storage-tank water heater keeps water warm 24/7, wasting a huge amount of energy. With no storage tank, a tankless water heater (also known as a demand type or instantaneous water heater) heats water only on the way to the faucet. Cold water circulates through a series of coils heated by either electric or gas heat. The heating element turns on only when a hot water faucet opens. With no tank to refill, water can be continuously heated, providing a constant flow of hot water.

Electric units provide hot water at a rate of two to five gallons per minute, depending on the model. Gas-fired units produce higher flow rates than electric ones, although the pilot light, if left on continuously, wastes energy. Also, more than one tankless unit may be required to provide enough hot water for a family. Tankless units generally cost more than a typical forty-gallon water heater but usually have longer warranties, last longer, and use less energy, saving money over the life of the tank. A storage-type water heater lasts between ten and fifteen years whereas a tankless heater can last more than twenty years. ENERGY STAR estimates that a typical family saves $100 or more per year with an ENERGY STAR–qualified tankless water heater.

# HILLMAN CITY
# SOLAR FARMHOUSE

PANELIZED

**PHOTOGRAPHER**
Shelly Borga/Dakota and Company (unless
otherwise noted)
(www.dakotaandco.com)

**DESIGNER/MANUFACTURER**
Deltec Homes, Inc.
(www.deltechomes.com)

**BUILDER**
Matthew Robinson
(matt@remodelprosnw.com)

**LOCAL DESIGNER/CODE CONSULTANT**
Matthew Smith
Dream Design Build
(http://dreamdesignbuild.org)

**INTERIOR DESIGNER**
Jenna Maenhout
Styled Out West
(https://www.styledoutwest.com)

**SIZE**
1,950 square feet

**LOCATION**
Seattle, Washington

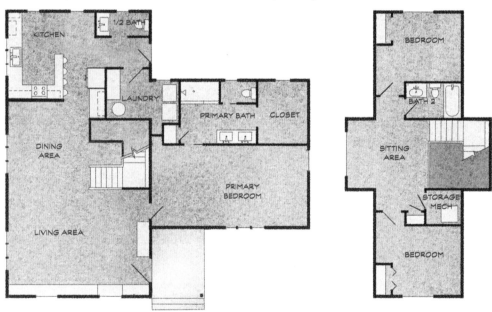

The owners of this house tore down their existing 1948 cottage, which was 700 square feet, and opted to build their new house on that site. They knew it was time for a larger house when they were expecting their first child and they added a second dog to the family. They entertained several ideas for adding on to their older house or remodeling it. Eventually they realized a tear-down/rebuild was the right decision for their growing family. Today they have two children and two dogs.

**Below:** The house was built to be not just very efficient but also low maintenance with a prepainted polymer poly-ash siding and a standing seam roof. Solar panels on the roof provide all the energy required to run the house.

## GREEN FEATURES

- Mold and termite resistant treatment on structural components
- Metal roof with recycled metal
- Locally sourced items
- No natural gas in house
- Repurposed and preowned furnishings

## ENERGY FEATURES

- Advanced insulation
- Ductless mini-split system
- Energy recovery ventilator (ERV)
- Solar panels
- ENERGY STAR appliances

# FINDING JUST THE RIGHT DESIGN

The couple started their research by simply searching for farmhouses. They stumbled upon prefab construction methods and decided that was how they wanted their house built, mainly because of its speed and efficiency. They then contacted various prefab companies and chose Deltec's panelized system. They were impressed with the company's commitment to renewable energy and the environmental impact of their construction—two factors that were high on the couple's priority list for selecting a company to build their home. They were also impressed that Deltec's facility uses 100 percent renewable energy and produces 80 percent less waste than for traditional homes. When they met with their representative, most of their priorities were met with the description of the company's solar farmhouse plan. They wanted an open floor plan, high energy efficiency, large windows, and high ceilings.

**Opposite:** The wainscoting in the living area is in keeping with the farmhouse design. All the vast cabinetry was custom built for the house.

**Right and below:** The house has extensive cabinetry, providing an abundance of storage.

## GETTING THE HOUSE BUILT

The couple worked closely with Deltec on the design. The company was very responsive and helpful with the couple's requests, and the construction went a lot smoother than they expected. The largest setbacks were delays because of COVID-19 and meeting city requirements. It took less than six months for Deltec to finalize plans to meet city codes. The build only took a few months, and the house was complete from tear-down to move-in in just eight months.

Matthew Smith, their designer, played a significant role from the very beginning of their project, and handled all the tedious items. The couple says "they could not have done any of this without his knowledge, patience, and guidance."

**Top:** The farmhouse look of the house is carried through in the kitchen with the sink and cabinetry. All the appliances are ENERGY STAR rated.

**Bottom:** The black wrought iron railing was custom designed for the owners by their designer Matthew Smith.

**Left:** An open shower in the primary bathroom satisfies the owners' desire for "locker-room style." The owners wanted to be able to just step quickly into the shower.

**Below:** The upstairs primary bedroom has several windows to provide lots of natural light and ventilation.

## OUTDOOR SPACE

The property does not provide a lot of outdoor space, but the new decking that wraps around their hot tub works well for them. They also have an open style pergola where they can enjoy looking up at the stars. The deck is partially covered, enabling the couple to grill on a rainy day. They are working to establish a garden and play area for their children, and they say they just love their new home.

**Above:** The front porch is an inviting entry into the house and provides a place to relax in the pleasant weather.

**Right:** A panel is being transported to the construction site. Photo courtesy of Deltec Homes, Inc.

# FRAMEGUARD TREATMENT

After being exposed to the elements, many houses can develop mold, fungal decay, and termites. Treating those issues after the house is built can be expensive and difficult, so using products that protect the home during the build and for years after makes sense. FrameGuard, a formula that must be applied in a factory setting by either spraying or dipping, is one method of pretreating the lumber. FrameGuard treatment offers both short- and long-term protection and ensures cleaner, brighter wood that is protected from its natural enemies. This protection can be especially important in areas that are prone to high humidity and extreme moisture. This treatment comes with a twenty-year warranty.

# THE RALEIGH SIMPLE HOME AND ADU COTTAGE

PANELIZED

PHOTOGRAPHER
Virtuance
(www.virtuance.com)

ARCHITECT/PANEL MANUFACTURER
Simple Homes
(www.simplehomes.com)

DEVELOPER/BUILDER
L&D Construction
(https://ldconstructiondenver.com)

SIZE
Primary House 1,520 square feet
Accessory Dwelling Unit 650 square feet

LOCATION
Denver, Colorado (West Colfax neighborhood)

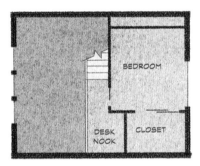

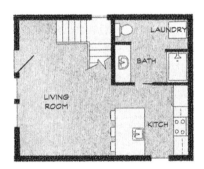

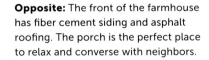

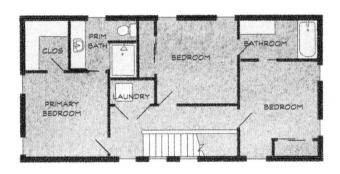

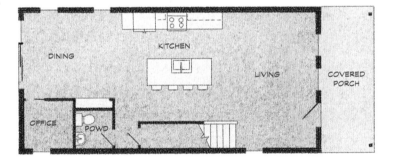

**Opposite:** The front of the farmhouse has fiber cement siding and asphalt roofing. The porch is the perfect place to relax and converse with neighbors.

One of the most sustainable features of this house, designed and panelized by Simple Homes, is that it is located on a lot where one single house once stood and where three homes plus two accessory dwelling units (ADUs) are now located. This is particularly important in areas like Denver and many other cities, where there is a shortage of housing and costs are too high for many local house hunters.

## GREEN FEATURES

- Metal roof on ADU made from recycled material
- No gas lines to house
- Added multiple housing to a one-house lot
- Induction ranges
- Reclaimed wood
- Low VOC paints and finishes
- Quartz countertops

## ENERGY FEATURES

- On-demand electric water heater
- Air-source heat pumps
- Energy recovery ventilator (ERV)
- ENERGY STAR appliances

## AIR TIGHTNESS

- 2.0 ACH

# THE COMPANY'S EFFICIENCY PLAN

L&D Construction, the developer and builder of the house, along with Simple Homes, the panelizer, established their company with the goal of building not only more sustainable housing but also better housing with less waste, using panelization. Simple Home's 20,000-square-foot factory is based in a former rail yard in Denver. The company states they have reduced the amount of wasted material in the framing process by up to 15 percent, and they have reduced construction time for the framing by 75 percent compared to on-site building.

**Above:** The living room area is in the front portion of the house. All the flooring throughout the first level of the house is solid hardwood.

**Top:** The stairs lead up to the three bedrooms and two bathrooms on the second floor.

**Bottom:** The kitchen is in the center of this open floor plan. The stove is induction and the refrigerator is ENERGY STAR rated.

## SIMPLE SHELL FRAMING METHOD

Simple Homes designed the house and ADU utilizing their Simple Shell building system: constructing panels comprised of wood studs, engineered wood, trusses, joists, installed windows, and exterior sheathing with an integrated weather barrier. These components are all coordinated with 3D modeling software to ensure accuracy, minimize waste, and save time. With this panelized building system, on-site assembly took only four hours for this house and ADU.

Components are assembled into a series of flat panels in the factory, up to ten feet tall and forty feet long. When completed, the panels are loaded onto a truck, delivered to the site, and installed with a crane. Joints between panels are sealed, and this weather-protected building envelope is then ready for interior work and the completion of the exterior. The houses can be weather tight and ready for mechanical, electrical, and plumbing (MEP) work in three to six days after they are set.

**Above:** The ADU at the rear of the main house has black Douglas fir siding with nontoxic pine tar paint finish.

**Opposite, top left:** The kitchen of the ADU has an induction cooktop, ENERGY STAR refrigerator, quartz countertops, and custom wood cabinets.

**Opposite, top right:** A work area is tucked into the second floor of the ADU.

**Opposite, bottom:** The stair treads and the main beam for the second floor of the ADU is a salvaged piece of Douglas fir from one of the builder's previous projects.

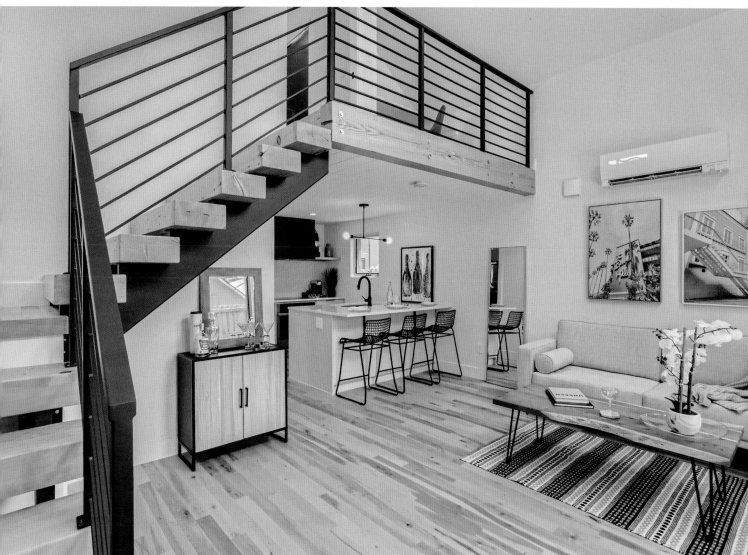

## CREATING AN EFFICIENT AND HEALTHY ENVIRONMENT

The house and ADU were built with no gas lines to the house. This is a safer way to heat and cool the house. Natural gas leaks can cause gas poisoning as well as fires and explosions. Even when functioning properly, gas cooking appliances can lead to poor indoor air quality. In addition, natural gas is considered bad for the environment since it is a non-renewable energy source, pollutes the air, and depletes the ozone layer.

Energy recovery ventilators (ERVs) are installed in both the house and ADU to provide continuous healthy air. They replace the stale air with the fresh outside air while maintaining the heat and cool already created in the house. Both structures were built very airtight, checked by a blower door test (see sidebar on page 17) with results that were 33 percent better than current International Energy Conservation Code (IECC). Both units also have on-demand electric hot water heaters and induction cooking ranges (see sidebar on page 173), which save energy.

David Shultz, the owner of L&D Construction and Simple Homes says, "We firmly believe that we should be building houses that last and perform for a minimum of one hundred years. To execute that, our company is highly focused on science building details (air leakage, water management, thermal comfort, and so on), with no gas lines coming into the house and choosing durable materials to ensure long-term comfort and performance for the housing we build."

**Above:** The house is one of three houses on the property where one house was demolished.

**Right:** The stovetop in the kitchen is induction.

# INDUCTION COOKING

Induction cooktops are more energy efficient, heat faster, and are more consistent than traditional electric ranges. With gas and traditional electric stoves, a good deal of the energy dissipates into the air and surrounding surfaces. With induction cooking, energy is supplied directly to the cooking vessel by the magnetic field, and almost all the source energy is transferred to that vessel. Induction cooktops contain copper coils beneath the cooking surface that receive an electric current, producing a magnetic field that induces current through ferrous (magnetic) pots. The currents heat the pots, and the cooktop remains relatively cool.

Induction cookers are easy to clean because the cooking surface is flat and smooth and does not get hot enough to make spilled food burn and stick. The burner shuts down automatically when iron or steel cookware is removed. This also means induction cooktops are safer than conventional units because there is less risk of burning fingers. These appliances require no gas lines, and a ductless hood eliminates the need for another opening in the exterior of the house.

With induction cooking, the pots must be compatible with the stovetop, which means you can only use pots made of magnetic materials. Other concerns are that the glass ceramic surface can be marred by a significant impact or scratched by sliding pots, and aluminum foil can melt onto the surface, permanently damaging the cooktop.

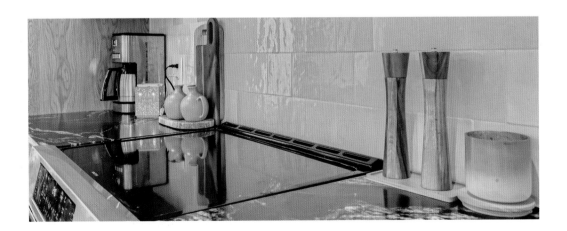

# LIPAN ROAD HOUSE

## MODULAR

**ARCHITECTS AND PHOTOS**
Rame and Russell Hruska
Intexure Architects
(www.intexure.com)

**MANUFACTURER/GENERAL CONTRACTOR**
Boxprefab
(https://boxprefab.com)

**SIZE**
Primary House, 1,847 square feet
Accessory dwelling unit, 600 square feet

**LOCATION**
Houston, Texas

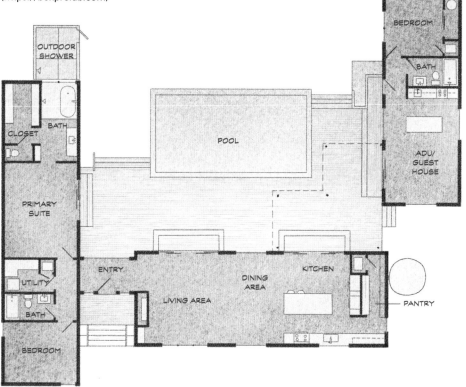

The owners of this house, empty-nester couple Peter and Linda Draper, operate a preschool adjacent to their property, creating a live-work situation with accessibility. Rather than a traditional neighborhood setting, this area is a mix of residential, commercial, and industrial buildings. Although so close to the school and other buildings, privacy for their home was still a goal.

The layout of the home includes an ADU, which provides space for extended family visits. The couples' long-term plan is to have their daughter one day occupy the main house while they downsize to the ADU, allowing them to age in place and extend the time they can remain in their home.

**Below:** The front façade of the house has fiber cement siding, which requires minimal maintenance. The house was sited on the property to minimize the removal of any trees.

## GREEN FEATURES

- Rainwater harvesting
- Low VOC materials
- Low-flow plumbing
- Drip irrigation; native and drought-tolerant plants
- Helical pier system
- Flood resiliency
- Universal Design

## ENERGY FEATURES

- Spray foam insulation
- Thermally broken, high performance low-E aluminum windows
- Solar ready
- ENERGY STAR appliances
- Smart, high efficiency heating, ventilation, and air conditioning
- LED lighting and controls
- Programmable thermostat
- Optimal orientation

## BUILDING MODULAR

It took six months to complete this house after it was set. COVID-19 and related supply chain issues were the cause of the delays. Rame Hruska, coarchitect and owner of Boxprefab, says the company has refined their process to reduce the on-site time and they expect a project such as this one will take less than four weeks on-site for future projects. Minimizing on-site work, they say, is really the key to their process and maximizes the benefits of off-site construction.

The Hruskas say this modular home is inherently more sustainable than a site-built house because it produced less waste in their factory's controlled environment and ultimately had less impact on the site. Because the structure didn't get wet during construction, there is less risk of potential mold and toxins, which are big issues with site-built construction in the Texas climate. The controlled environment at the factory also allows air ventilation, improving indoor air quality to the finished home.

**Above:** The living room, dining area, and kitchen are all open and have multiple, carefully placed windows and doors to create a light, bright open feeling while carefully screening views and maintaining privacy. The fireplace runs on gas.

# DESIGNING AN EFFICIENT AND SUSTAINABLE HOUSE

The home was carefully sited on a small grove of existing mature trees and opens up to the north with natural light and views, maximizing cooling loads in Houston's hot climate. Operable windows encourage air flow and capture prevailing breezes. Rainwater harvesting captures water from both the main house and ADU and is used in the drip irrigation system.

**Right:** The rainwater harvesting tank provides water for the landscaping, reducing stormwater runoff.

**Below:** Appliances in the kitchen are all ENERGY STAR rated. The countertops are quartz, and the drawers of the cabinets are full extension slides on drawers for easy access.

**Top:** At the rear of the house are multiple doors leading out to the pool. A glass wall connects the social and bedroom areas of the house. The outdoor living space serves as the center of the home, connecting the three modules. The two modules of the main house form an L-shape home with the detached ADU providing a U-shaped feel, connected through decking and landscape elements, and embracing the outdoor spaces and a pool.

**Bottom:** The main bathroom has a Japanese-style shower and bathtub for a relaxing soak and a clean-off shower in the same location. The shower opens with a sliding door to a private outdoor space, which embraces a large sycamore tree and brings nature into the bathing experience.

## PLANNING FOR THE FUTURE

The helical pier foundation (see sidebar on page 181) adds flexibility to the owners for the future. The prefab construction of the house is also designed so that additional modules can be added to the structure as the homeowners' needs change.

**Top:** Like the main house, the ADU has multiple windows in this kitchen and living space.

**Bottom:** The modules are delivered to the site where they will be set on the helical pier foundation.

**Above:** The ADU is not attached to the main house but helps create the U-shape around the pool.

## CREATING A FOREVER HOME

The architects incorporated Universal Design elements to the house so it can be the owners' forever home. The goal was to extend livability for aging in place but without going to full ADA (Americans with Disabilities Act) requirements. The house has extra maneuvering space and clear floor space in the primary bathroom to make sure there is ample room for mobility assistance devices, if necessary. The house has light, bright finishes to aid visibility. Additional features include lever-style door hardware and lever-style plumbing fixtures, a low threshold shower (although it still has a small step), slip-resistant, transition-less flooring as much as possible, a side gate that provides access with fewer steps to the main floor level, and steps that can be converted to a small ramp. There are full extension slides on drawers in the kitchen, and programable and phone-controlled smart lighting and thermostats.

This house was created to be a perfect house for the Drapers today and into the future.

# HELICAL PIER FOUNDATION

Helical, or spiral, piers are manufactured steel foundation pins that are driven (or screwed) into the soil to a depth below the frost line using hydraulic machinery.

These systems are often used as a fix for sinkholes—helical piers can be screwed either into the adjacent stronger soil or into the stronger soil below the weak sinkhole pocket. They can also be driven to greater depths than traditional foundations can be dug.

The cost of installing a helical pier system is more expensive than a traditional foundation with concrete footings, but the benefits can outweigh the costs—installation occurs in one day with very little disruption to the site and surrounding property.

Although the owners of this house are committed to this location and plan to be in this home long term, having this type of foundation gives them flexibility, allowing the home to be moved rather than demolished if the clients' needs or urban conditions change. To relocate a house, the utilities are disconnected, the "screws" are removed, and the house is then hoisted onto the back of a flat-bed trailer, with little evidence that the house was even there. (The helical piers can even be reused.) Another advantage is the speed and security that this type of foundation allows, especially in Houston where soils are known to have movement because of all the rain and expansive* soils. No soil reports need to be filed before the helical pier foundation can be set, and, since helical piers don't require the cure time of concrete, they can be installed in even wet conditions, enhancing the prefab process.

---

*Expansive soils consist primarily of fine clay particles that absorb a lot of rainwater, increasing the soil volume. This propensity to swell and shrink causes ground movement and is a problem for foundations in the Houston area. The soil is often called "gumbo clay."

# HILL HOUSE

## POST AND BEAM/PANELIZED

**GENERAL CONTRACTOR**
Homeowner

**ARCHITECT/MANUFACTURER**
Yankee Barn Homes
(https://yankeebarnhomes.com)

**INTERIOR DESIGNER**
Michael Maher Design
(www.michaelmaherdesign.com)

**SIZE**
2,061 square feet

**LOCATION**
Dorset, Vermont

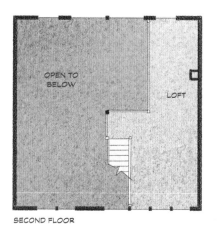

SECOND FLOOR

FIRST FLOOR

After having grown up in Ohio and then living in Florida for several years, Kelle and Dan Lloyd decided to move to Vermont and build their forever home. While searching for the right area, they visited Merck Forest and Farmland nature preserve and saw the mountain views over Dorset and knew that this was their place. They were able to purchase 280 acres with the exact view they fell in love with, on the Taconic Mountain Range with views of the Green Mountain Range.

**Below:** The architectural design of the house is mid-century modern with a shed roof, high ceilings, lots of glass, and relatively sparse interiors. Exterior siding of the house is tigerwood.

## GREEN FEATURES

- Low-flow faucets and showerheads
- Central vacuum
- Well water
- Locally sourced materials

## ENERGY FEATURES

- Super insulation
- All LED lighting
- Heat recovery ventilation system
- Hybrid water heater
- Hydronic radiant floor heating
- Wood burning stove with soapstone
- Photovoltaic panels
- Ductless mini-split heat pumps
- Spray foam insulation in the lower level

# CHOOSING TO BUILD A POST AND BEAM HOME

The couple wanted to build a prefabricated house because they liked the idea of the walls and roof being constructed indoors, safe from the elements. An additional benefit was the simultaneous building of the foundation and components of the house, which would save them time. They visited several timber frame/post and beam builders, but upon meeting Yankee Barn Home's design project manager, they felt she understood their vision and could help them through the design process. They also preferred YBH's energy efficient method of construction.

**Opposite:** The wood stove in the living area provides extra heat on cold days. Their neighbor and friend, interior designer Michael Maher, helped the couple locate several mid-century antiques such as the Turkish patchwork area rugs and teak table lamp.

**Right:** The gracious entrance to the house has two mid-century modern George III-style "Cock Fighting" chairs and floating staircases with tigerwood treads and railings, which go up to the loft and down to the basement.

**Below:** The kitchen is open to the living area, with an overhanging loft. All the lights in the house are LEDs.

## PRIORITIES FOR THEIR NEW HOME

Kelle and Dan began their design process by evaluating the minimum square footage they needed and wanted for each room. Over the years they had discovered that a dining room and a formal living room were a waste of space for them, and they decided to eliminate those rooms. They wanted to build a modern, mid-century-style mountain home, with the view being the focal point upon entering the house.

Although they were building a post and beam house, they wanted it to look and feel modern with lots of glass. With a twenty-foot-high wall of mostly glass and nine-and-a-half-foot-tall glass doors, the view is part of the house. All the vertical supports are hidden in the walls with only two visible posts supporting the loft.

**Above:** The couple say sitting in the hot tub or having a cocktail by the firepit is always a joy. They can look one way to appreciate their beautiful view or back toward their house to enjoy their dream home.

**Right:** The rear wall of the house is glass, allowing for beautiful views of the mountains beyond. The precut post and beams are made of Douglas fir. The marble behind and under the wood stove is Danby Marble from the Danby Marble quarry just minutes away from their home.

## BUILDING IN ENERGY EFFICIENCY

The couple also wanted a well-insulated home, but they did not want to limit the size of the windows or ceiling height, which can sometimes be vehicles for heat loss. By using LED lighting and other energy efficient systems such as heat pumps, radiant heating (see sidebar on page 190), and forty-eight solar panels, they were able to have the design they wanted and still have a very efficient home.

**Opposite, top:** The primary bedroom has windows on two sides to make the room feel one with the exterior. Double-glass doors lead out to the front yard.

**Opposite, bottom:** The primary bathroom, off the bedroom, opens to the exterior. All the fixtures in the bathroom are low flow.

**Below:** This mid-century modern house sits on 280 acres, nestled in the greenery of the Taconic Mountain Range with views of the Green Mountain Range. The home is located approximately half of a mile from the road. The views of the mountains and trees are all they see from their home; no neighboring homes can be seen from their home and vice versa.

## CHALLENGES IN CONSTRUCTION

While clearing the land for the house, the couple discovered a rock ledge. They had to blast the area to break it up but were able to use the blasted material for the base of the driveway and for landscaping the stone walls and steps.

It took the couple ten months from clearing trees and breaking ground to moving in, which was just days before the COVID-19 shutdown. They say their favorite things about the house are the beautiful views they can see from their house, the privacy the house affords them, and the excellent use of all the space that fits their lifestyle. Having been directly involved in every aspect from design, build, to completion gives them confidence that it was built exactly as they wanted it.

# RADIANT HEAT: HYDRONIC AND ELECTRIC

Radiant heat is becoming an increasingly popular heating alternative, providing clean, even heat, and warming objects in the room rather than the air as forced hot air systems do. Radiant systems provide greater comfort as heat is spread evenly throughout the area. The system can be zoned so only the areas being used are heated, increasing efficiency. With radiant heat, no particulates and pollutants are forced into the environment, unlike forced hot air systems. Additionally, the system is noise free. Radiant heating systems are imbedded in flooring, ceiling, or wall panels and can even be used to melt snow on driveways and sidewalks. Hydronic or hot water radiant systems can also heat domestic hot water.

There are two types of radiant heat—electric and hydronic. Though they basically work the same way, installations are vastly different and operating costs are different as well. Hydronic systems are more complicated to install because they require controllers with pumps and special PEX tubing to circulate water heated by an electric, gas-fired, or oil-fired high efficiency boiler.

Because they do not require high temperatures to operate, these hydronic systems can be interfaced with thermal solar collectors, ground source geothermal heat pumps, or air-to-water heat pumps. Hydronic systems are more expensive to install but less expensive to operate. Electric systems are easier and less expensive to install but more expensive to operate, making them often impractical for heating an entire house but effective for small areas, such as bathrooms.

One disadvantage of some radiant systems is they take longer to heat up an area than other types of systems. One type of hydronic system is PEX tubing embedded in concrete which acts as a heat sink, absorbing the heat first, before the room gets it. Depending on how large the heat sink is (such as a cold foundation), this could take a bit of time. Once the heat is turned off, the heat sink will take a similarly long time to dissipate the heat, keeping the area warm for a longer time. These types of concrete radiant (large mass) systems can have a heat delivery effect of overdelivering the heat due to the large amount of heat that is stored in the concrete, meaning the heat from the concrete will keep delivering even when it's not needed. Another very popular type√ of hydronic radiant is aluminum panel systems that use no concrete. These panel systems don't have the heat sink characteristic; they use aluminum to conduct heat and are much faster to heat up and cool down.

The hydronic radiant heating system in the Hill House was supplied by Warmboard and installed by the homeowners. They personally placed all the floor panels and tubing for the system. The sleek, efficient, and wireless boiler made this system particularly attractive to them, along with the ability to update the system remotely.

**Below:** The solar panels are free standing in the front yard of the house. The house is connected to the power grid (Green Mountain Power), but the solar panels provide all the power the couple needs for their home and more. They say the excess is issued as a credit, which they use towards their vacation rental home. The radiant heat boiler uses propane to heat the water for the radiant floor system in the house.

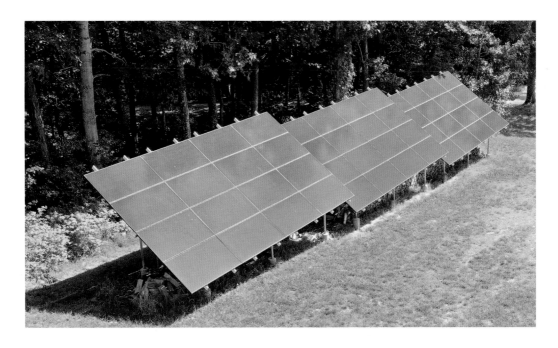

# HIVE HOUSE

### MODULAR

**PHOTOGRAPHER**
Adam Powers
(http://adamcpowers.com)

**ARCHITECTURAL DESIGNER**
Chris Herlihy
Polestar Design
(www.polestar.com)

**ARCHITECT OF RECORD**
Kevin Browne Architecture

**GENERAL CONTRACTOR**
Schiavi Custom Builders
(https://schiavicustom.com)

**MANUFACTURER**
KBS
(www.kbsbuildersinc.com)

**LANDSCAPE ARCHITECT**
Soren Deniord Design Studio
(www.sorendeniord.com)

**SIZE**
1,905 square feet

**LOCATION**
Scarborough, Maine

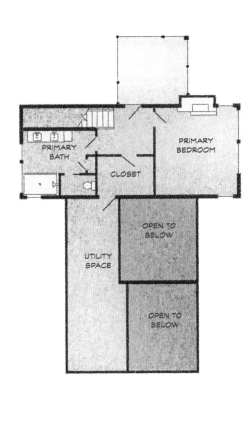

**Opposite:** The house is on pillars to allow native blueberry grasses to retake the ground underneath. Since the house is next to wetlands, the gravel auto court allows water to seep back into the ground. The exterior of the house is cedar with a Corten steel frame.

The owners of this house wanted an eco-friendly, energy efficient house that was private and comfortable. They were lucky to find nineteen beautiful acres prior to the COVID-19 pandemic hit, before land became more difficult to attain. Working with their designer, Chris Herlihy, they created a home with a small footprint, an open concept interior, lofty cathedral ceilings, and large multiple windows to enjoy the surrounding forest.

## GREEN FEATURES

- Locally sourced materials
- Charging station
- Native landscaping
- Low-flow plumbing fixtures
- Induction stove

## ENERGY FEATURES

- Solar panels
- Battery backup system
- Passive solar design
- Radiant concrete flooring with heat pump
- LED lighting
- Triple-glazed windows
- Super insulation

## BUILDING MODULAR

The couple built their home modular because they were advised that it would be a more efficient way to build. Being environmentally conscious they were also attracted to the fact that their house would be built in a factory, with far less waste created.

**Opposite:** The ceilings and the interior walls are native, white-washed pine. The flooring is concrete, which works particularly well with their hydronic radiant heating system and also provides a clean, modern look.

**Right:** An induction stove is both attractive and avoids the need for a gas line into the house.

**Below:** The kitchen has all high efficiency appliances in addition to the induction stove. Midnight blue concrete panels were used for the backsplash, bird's-eye maple for the raised countertop, and porcelain for the other countertops.

**Left:** The interior and exterior railings are composed of modern cable rails.

**Opposite:** The dining area is just off the living room and creates a very open concept for the social space of the house. It also doubles as a dance hall where the couple can swing dance, with the chandelier raised out of the way via a pulley system.

## ENERGY EFFICIENCY AS A PRIORITY

All the decisions made for the house were geared toward building an energy efficient house. The solar panels currently provide most of the energy needed to run the house. The couple says they plan to add thirty more panels, which will make the house net zero. Through the local electric company, they will be able to donate the extra power the panels will create to those who need it. The couple have a one-car garage with a charging station which they use to fuel their electric car.

The house is heated and cooled with a hydronic heat pump radiant heating system (see sidebar on page 190), which is an efficient and comfortable type of heating. A heat pump is used for cooling the house and providing additional heat when necessary for the very cold Maine days. Because the house was built tight and with triple-pane windows, there is an energy recovery ventilation (ERV) system to keep the air in the house fresh and healthy.

## RESPECT FOR THE ENVIRONMENT

The owners of this house took many steps to respect the land and the environment. The house is set on pillars to tread lightly on the site and so nature can return where it can. Since the house is next to wetlands, the pea stone auto court allows for minimal disturbance of the surrounding environment. One of the owners of the house is a beekeeper and maintains five hives, even throughout the difficult cold winters. He does it to "do something positive for the world" and, as an additional advantage, his friends enjoy the honey.

There is no drywall in the house on the walls or the ceiling, and there are natural components throughout. No gas lines come into the house, so the house operates mostly on solar energy and electricity from the grid when it is needed.

**Opposite, top:** The guest bathroom with entrances from the guest room and entry has a cedar ceiling, and the walls are painted poplar.

**Opposite, bottom:** The sitting room doubles as a guest room with a wall system that lowers to reveal a bed.

**Above:** The primary bedroom has a Vermont blue stone wall, which disguises the flue, an extension of the fireplace below. The designer, Chris Herlihy, created a beautiful shelving unit with the stone.

**Right:** Floor to ceiling porcelain tile adorns the primary bathroom on the second floor. Multiple windows in the room bring in a large amount of natural light.

**Above:** A large deck off the rear of the house completes the first floor. A barely visible screen surrounds the deck off the primary bedroom on the second floor, allowing the owners to enjoy a bug-free outdoor experience.

**Left:** The entrance to the house is recessed to provide a sheltered and welcoming approach.

# TRIPLE-PANE
# (OR GLAZED) WINDOWS

Triple-pane windows are helping home-owners meet the high level of efficiency being sought for many houses today. These windows have three layers of glass hermetically sealed with an inert gas—either argon or krypton—trapped between the layers. Low-E coatings can be applied on the panes, further hindering heat transfer and providing additional efficiency. Reduced heating and cooling costs, increased comfort, and reduced noise pollution are advantages to triple-pane windows. The main deterrent to using these windows is the higher initial cost, which can vary depending on the windows being used, but this increased cost is recouped over time through energy savings.

Here are three ratings to consider when evaluating windows:

- U-factor—This term refers to the rate of energy loss through windows and doors. The lower the U-factor, the better the window insulates. This rating ranges from 0.12 to 1.20.
- SHGC (solar heat gain coefficient)—This measures how much solar radiant energy is admitted through a window or door. The SHGC is expressed as a number between 0 and 1, the fraction of the heat from the sun that enters through the window glass. The lower the number, the less solar radiation it transmits; the higher the number, the more it transmits.
- VT (visual transmittance)—This is an optical property that indicates the amount of visible light transmitted through the window or door. VT is a number between 0 and 1; the higher the VT, the more light is transmitted.

The triple-pane windows on the Hive House are by Anderson.

# MARIS ADU

## KIT HOME

**PHOTOGRAPHERS**
Cindy Apple (www.cindyapple.com),
unless otherwise noted

**PLANNING AND DESIGN**
Michael Harris
Warmmodern Living
(https://warmmodernliving.com)

**MANUFACTURER**
Lindal Cedar Homes
(https://lindal.com)

**SIZE**
984 square feet

**LOCATION**
Seattle, Washington

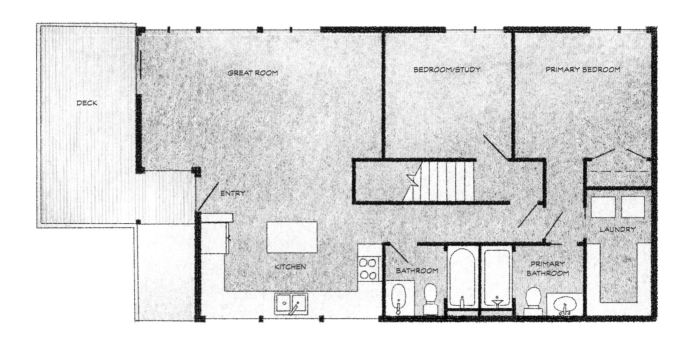

**Opposite:** The exterior siding of the ADU is fiber cement with tight knot cedar at the front and entry. The house was pushed back on the property beyond the edge, so a lower level could be built to include windows and sliding doors to the rear on that level. Photo courtesy of Michael Harris.

Amy and Frank Soto, owners of the main house, built the ADU with their original intent to provide housing for either their adult daughter and her family as a starter home or for Amy's parents, but they both declined the offer. So, the Sotos decided to use it as a rental property.

## GREEN FEATURES

- Low-flow faucets
- Minimal excavation
- Fiber cement siding
- No VOCs
- Quartz countertops

## ENERGY FEATURES

- Charging station
- Mini-split heat pumps
- High efficiency windows and doors
- Strategic placement of windows
- ENERGY STAR appliances and light fixtures
- Super insulation in walls and roofing
- Cross ventilation

## DECIDING TO BUILD A KIT HOUSE

The couple say they had no intention of using a kit house manufacturer for their new home, but when they met Michael Harris, an architectural designer and independent distributor for Lindal Cedar Homes, they were "overwhelmed by his knowledge and passion for home design." When they learned about the custom kit process of Lindal Cedar homes, it was a "bonus." They were impressed with the company because they were able to make modifications to the plan to meet their budget and they got a firm price for the house at the onset.

The ADU was built simultaneously with the main house, which saved them money and was another advantage of building their home with kit prefabrication. They initially planned to build a 500-square-foot structure but as their requirements for the ADU increased, it gradually grew larger, close to the maximum (1,000 square feet) allowed at 985 square feet. This allowed them to have one and a half bathrooms (later changed), so the primary suite had a private bathroom, a laundry area, and plenty of storage. They also opted to build a basement, which is an unfinished space.

**Opposite:** Ceiling beams in the living area add warmth and cohesiveness to this area. Clerestory windows bring in additional light along with the wall of windows on the south side of the room.

**Right:** There is a small eating area in the open floor plan. Two doors lead out adding accessibility as well as light with the porch door glass and the entrance door with glass insets.

**Below:** The appliances in the kitchen are ENERGY STAR rated. Clerestory windows in this area bring additional light and ventilation to the kitchen and beyond.

## THE ADU DESIGN

The ADU was designed with the same interior and exterior materials as their main house—the Sotos call the ADU their "baby house." They wanted this smaller house "to feel spacious and stylish without breaking the budget."

The layout of the ADU has changed since it was initially designed. The dining room was converted into a second bedroom, and the bathroom area was redesigned to have two full baths instead of the initial half bath. Amy and Frank are delighted with this new layout, which the renters also love. The renters "don't ever want to leave," and just installed a charging port for their new Tesla!

**Left:** Although the floor plan is petite, the open floor plan makes it feel more spacious than it is.

## A BONUS BASEMENT

The local ADU regulations limit the living area in ADUs to 1,000 square feet, but unfinished spaces, garages, and decks are not included in that 1,000-square-foot limit.

This entire site was a gently sloping hillside and, as with the primary home, the ADU was positioned to allow a full daylight basement. Since the basement cannot be finished, it serves as a terrific play area for the residents' kids during Seattle's rainy seasons or it could be a woodworking workshop or a practice studio for a "garage band."

## BUILDING THE ADU TO HIGH ENERGY STANDARDS

Energy efficiency was one of the owners' priorities. Harris designed the windows for maximum lighting and cross ventilation. The Sotos planned on installing solar panels, but the trees across the road were too tall and would have blocked them. They opted to use only electricity to power the house to avoid having gas lines coming into the house and they installed very efficient mini-split heat pumps (see sidebar on page 83) for heating and cooling and a heat pump water heater.

Amy and Frank plan to retire in about five years, spend time traveling, and then move into the ADU. They will then rent out the main house, which will be more than they need by then.

**Opposite, left:** The original dining area was converted to a bedroom to better suit the young couple who rented the ADU. This bedroom now serves as a nursery for the renters' baby.

**Opposite, right:** The original small powder room was converted to a full bathroom adding a shower/bath to this small room.

**Below:** The primary bedroom has a large window bringing in natural light and ventilation.

**Above:** The main house can be seen from the breezeway of the ADU. Photo courtesy of Patrick Barta.

**Left:** The outdoor porch extends the living space and is a comfortable place to relax.

# WHY ADUS?

Over the last several years there has been a big increase in the locations that permit ADUs and the number of them that are being built. An ADU is a self-contained residential dwelling on the same property as a single-family home that includes a kitchen, bathroom, and sleeping facility, is permanently affixed to the property, and usually has a separate entrance from the primary home. It can be built over the garage, in a converted part of the house, such as an altered basement, or as a freestanding unit on the property, such as where the garage once stood.

Most commonly ADUs are used for family members, such as adult children and elderly parents, but many are also used as rental units or "mortgage helpers" that bring needed rental housing into neighborhoods where rental buildings aren't allowed. ADUs are sometimes called granny flats, mother-in-law apartments, laneway houses, etc. They have become increasingly popular because they create more affordable housing and density without changing the nature of neighborhoods, as well as substantially raising the resale value of the home. However, they are dependent on local building codes, zoning laws, and permit requirements.

With the increase of people working at home, ADUs are often being built as offices to provide a quieter, more private place to work, which can also double as guesthouses. More recently, ADUs are being used as rental spaces to help offset the cost of running the larger house on the property. Some people have built ADUs so they can live in the ADU and rent out their bigger home. In resort areas, ADUs can serve as places for seasonal workers to rent while they are working in that location.

Most locations have restrictions on the look, size, and residents who can live in the ADUs. In some cities there are limitations on who can live in the ADU—for example, family members only—and in other locations, they can just be renters. Some cities require the property owner to live on-site. Limitations on size can depend on the size of the property, size of the primary house, and setbacks. Some cities require an extensive permit approval process including neighbor notification, or city council approval, while other cities keep it simple. The places with simpler permit approval processes have seen a much higher uptake in ADU construction.

# LOWRY HOUSE

## PANELIZED

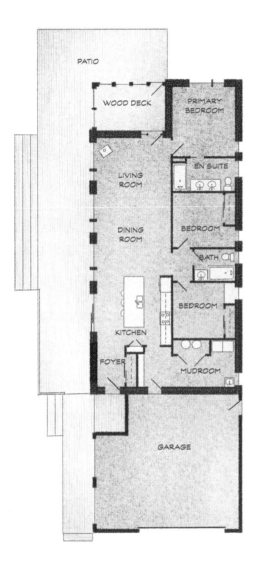

**PHOTOGRAPHER**
Thomas Heidman
(www.heidmandefinition.com)

**ARCHITECTURAL DESIGNER**
Mike Anderson
Passive Design Solutions
(www.passivedesign.ca)

**GENERAL CONTRACTOR/MANUFACTURER**
Ben Lowry
Lowry Building Company
(www.LowryBuilding.ca)

**SIZE**
1,601 square feet

**LOCATION**
Orillia, Ontario

**B**en Lowry started framing houses in high school. He later built straw bale houses, developed real estate in Toronto, and managed a mid-size commercial construction company for several years before deciding to start his own business building high performance prefabricated houses. The Lowry House became the prototype for houses he continues to build.

**Below:** The deep overhangs of this shed-style roof create a canopy that shelters this modern rectangular plan and provides good shade in the summer months keeping the house comfortable. It also allows for excellent solar heat gain in the winter that sinks right into the concrete flooring, slowly radiating heat during the night. The exterior of the house has standing seam metal that is sustainable and highly efficient. Although the roof and siding are both standing seam metal, the roof is black and the siding white.

## GREEN FEATURES

- High efficiency heat recovery ventilator
- Locally sourced materials
- Durable metal siding
- Engineered slab-on-grade foundation
- Low carbon wall panels with dense-packed cellulose insulation
- No gas lines into the house
- Induction stove

## ENERGY FEATURES

- Energy modeled with WUFI Passive
- Optimal solar orientation
- Triple-pane windows and doors
- Overhangs to prevent overheating
- Super insulated
- Air-source heat pump
- Concrete floors
- Hybrid hot water heater
- Solar ready

## AIR TIGHTNESS

- 0.52 ACH  (see sidebar on page 17)

## BUILDING WITH PANELIZATION

Lowry started thinking about prefab construction when he was in his early twenties building straw bale houses. He saw the huge opportunity to decrease the amount of labor time and material waste typical of on-site construction. He also became familiar with the advantages of 3D modeling software that allows him to prebuild the house virtually and then create cut lists and fabrication drawings that can effectively produce floor, wall, and roof panels in large sections.

**Opposite:** The spacious great room has high ceilings and clerestory windows facing south, bringing in lots of light and solar energy in the winter when it is needed. The 17-inch-thick, south-facing wall assembly provided the depth to create window seats all along the front wall.

**Right:** The flooring throughout the house is polished concrete. The air-source heat pump can be seen on the wall.

**Below:** The maple added character to the gable panels on the kitchen island.

## A FIRST VERY PASSIVE HOUSE

Lowry purchased the property, which is across the street from the house he grew up in, from his parents. He decided he wanted to build a house based on the standards of Passive House because "it is a great building standard based on rigorous building science, and is focused primarily on energy efficiency, indoor air quality, and overall comfort." (He has since built several other passive houses.)

He connected with Mike Anderson, at Passive Design Solutions (PDS), because of the company's depth of experience and pioneering work on passive house design in Canada. PDS was developing a suite of predesigned energy efficient plans that are perfect for prefabricated construction. These plans were far less expensive than full custom architectural design and had a much shorter timeline to completion.

Ben wanted to build a simple shaped bungalow house with three bedrooms and two bathrooms. He originally planned to sell the house when it was completed, but he is currently living in the house with his wife Gillian, nine-year-old daughter, seven-year-old son, and a dog, Bo. He says he has benefited greatly by seeing how the building performs firsthand. Ben planned to have the house PH certified but, with difficulty meeting the stringent requirements, he decided not to pursue certification. The house came very close to the levels required and even surpassed the air tightness metric (which is 0.06 ACH@ 50 pascals.)

Passive Design Solutions did the energy modeling and optimization for this stock design using WUFI Passive modeling software. This software shows how altering different components will alter the energy performance and achieve optimal energy functioning. For example, the angle of the

**Opposite:** A screened porch expands the livable area of the house for most of the year.

**Right, top:** The wood stove serves as a primary source of heat in the winter. Lowry says he burns about a bush cord each season, which is minimal for this climate.

**Right, bottom:** A large part of the primary bathroom is tiled. The room was kept a stark white except for the black faucets.

sun was modeled at different times of the year to better understand how the depth and angle of the roof overhang on the southeast facing tall wall would affect solar heat gain during the winter versus the summer. In this way, the house retains free heat during the winter months but is well shaded through the summer. Energy costs for Lowry's house is about ninety dollars a month, several hundred dollars less than the average house in Canada.

## UTILIZING LOCAL MATERIALS

When he was working on the interior finishes of the project, Lowry was able to use the hardwoods that he had been harvesting from his family farm for years. Windowsills and kitchen island paneling were all milled and fabricated by Lowry using this wood. The exterior cedar on the screened porch, front entry, and deck are eastern white cedar harvested and milled in nearby Tobermory, Ontario.

Lowry says this house was his prototype for panelization and passive house construction, both of which he wanted to test at his own home. It has surpassed his initial expectations. He will now continue to use the methods and materials he chose for this house for future construction projects. He looks forward to working with PDS in the future.

**Top:** The aerial view shows the house's proximity to Lake Couchiching, where the family is able to swim in the warmer months.

**Bottom:** A grassy sitting area and firepit are at the rear of the house.

# HEAT PUMP CLOTHES DRYER

When homeowners are trying to save energy, using a heat pump clothes dryer, rather than a conventional one, is a great option, since clothes dryers are one of the biggest consumers of energy in a home. According to ENERGY STAR, heat pump clothes dryers can reduce energy usage by at least 28 percent.

These units are closed-loop systems, recycling the heated warm air that is used to remove moisture from the clothes. The warm air goes through an evaporator to remove the moisture without losing too much of the heat and is then reused. Instead of releasing the warm humid air through a vent to the outside as a conventional condenser dryer does, the air is recirculated and the water is drained into a water tank, that must be manually drained, or it can be drained via a hose automatically into a pipe that goes to a sink, drainpipe, or dedicated floor drain. One of the important aspects of these dryers is that without a vent, for a dryer (or bathroom vent or range hood), air tightness is preserved.

In addition to the energy savings, heat pump dryers dry clothes at a lower temperature, making them gentler on clothes. They are also easy to install since they don't require ventilation. They take just a short time longer than conventional dryers to dry clothes. They are also better for the environment since they use far less energy and ultimately save money. Compact models are particularly useful in small houses and ADUs as they don't require a vent and can be placed in any room where there is a water source and electricity. All ENERGY STAR-certified models include a moisture sensor that turns off the machine when the clothes are dry, saving time and energy. Several brands today sell ENERGY STAR-certified heat pump dryers including Whirlpool, which is in the Lowry House.

# SUPPLIERS

## ASHFORD WEEHOUSE

Andersen Windows (windows)
www.andersenwindows.com

Azure Wine Fridge
https://azurehomeproducts.
com

LifeBreath (heat recovery
ventilator)
www.lifebreath.com/us/

LG (washer and dryer)
www.lg.com/us/

Miele (appliances)
www.mieleusa.com

Taylor Metals (siding)
https://taylormetal.com

WD Flooring (flooring)
www.wdflooring.com

Wolf (range and vent hood)
www.subzero-wolf.com

Goodman (split-system heat
pump)
www.goodmanmfg.com

Winger Woodworking
(cabinetwork)
San Jacinto, California

LP Flameblock (fire-resistant
sheathing)
https://lpcorp.com

## CONEXUS HOUSE

Frigidaire (refrigerator and
stove)
www.frigidaire.com

Kohler (plumbing fixtures)
www.us.kohler.com/us/

Marvin Windows
www.marvin.com

Meganite (countertops)
www.meganite.com

Mr. Cool (mini-split HVAC
system)
https://mrcool.com

Timbertech (composite
decking)
www.timbertech.com

## COWBOY MODERN
## DESERT ECO-RETREAT

All Modern (furnishings)
www.allmodern.com

Caesarstone (quartz
countertop)
www.caesarstoneus.com

Cavaliere (oven hood)
www.cavalierehoods.com

CB2 (wardrobe)
www.cb2.com

Crate and Barrel (furnishings)
www.crateandbarrel.com

EQ3 (furnishings)
www.eq3.com

Glacier Bay (toilets)
www.homedepot.com

IKEA (furnishings and
cabinetry)
www.ikea.com

Jacuzzi (spa)
www.jacuzzi.com

KitchenAid (oven/range,
refrigerator, dishwasher)
www.kitchenaid.com

Kräus (sink and faucets)
www.kraususa.com

Milgard (high performance
windows and doors)
www.milgard.com

Minka Aire (ceiling fans with
lights)
www.minkagroup.net

Nest (smart thermostat)
https://nest.com

Oxygen (exterior lighting)
https://www.oxygen.
lighting/collections/
oxygen-outdoor-lighting-fans

Urban Outfitters (furnishings)
www.urbanoutfitters.com

West Elm (furnishings)
www.westelm.com

## GOOD VIBES HOUSE

Caesarstone (kitchen
countertops)
www.caesarstoneus.com

Daltile (tile)
www.daltile.com

Garrison Collection (wood
flooring)
www.garrisoncollection.com

GE (washer and dryer)
www.geappliances.com

IKEA (cabinets)
www.ikea.com

Milgard (windows and doors)
www.milgard.com

Samsung (air handler)
www.samsunghvac.com

Schoolhouse (bathroom and
kitchen light fixtures)
www.schoolhouse.com

Whirlpool (kitchen appliances)
www.whirlpool.com

## HARRISON LANE HOUSE

Aqua Brass (plumbing fixtures)
https://aquabrass.com/en

Fir-Stone Inc. (quartz countertops)
www.fir-stone.com

Fisher & Paykel (refrigerator)
www.fisherpaykel.com

Gorenje (washer and dryer)
www.gorenje.com

Lotus LED Lights
www.lotusledlights.com

Luminaire Authentik (lighting fixture)
www.luminaireauthentik.com/en/

Lifebreath (heat recovery ventilator)
www.lifebreath.com

Porter & Charles (convection oven and gas range)
www.porterandcharles.ca

Popham Design (tiles)
www.pophamdesign.com

Vetta Windows
www.vettawindows.com

## HILL HOUSE

Blue Star (refrigerator and range)
www.bluestarcooking.com

Fujitsu (mini-split air conditioners)
www.fujitsugeneral.com/us

Hearthstone (wood stove)
www.hearthstonestoves.com

Lifebreath (heat recovery ventilator)
www.lifebreath.com

Marvin Windows and Doors (fiberglass/wood windows and doors)
www.marvin.com

Vent-A-Hood (exhaust hood)
www.ventahood.com

Viewrail (floating tigerwood treads and railings)
www.viewrail.com

Warmboard (boiler and radiant floor panels)
www.warmboard.com

## HILLMAN CITY SOLAR FARMHOUSE

Boral (pre-painted, vertical, poly-ash [polymer and fly-ash] siding)
www.boral.com

Broan (energy recovery ventilator)
www.broan-nutone.com

FrameGuard (mold and termite resistant treatment on structural components)
www.wolmanizedwood.com

LG (mini-split system)
https://lghvac.com

Marvin Integrity (windows)
www.marvin.com

Solterra Solar (solar panels)
https://solar.solterra.com

## HIVE HOUSE

Anderson (windows and doors)
www.andersenwindows.com

AO Smith (heat pump hot water heater)
www.aosmith.com

Daikin (heat pumps for cooling and heating)
https://daikincomfort.com

Dekton (porcelain kitchen countertop)
www.dekton.com

DXV (plumbing fixtures)
www.dxv.com/en

Feeney (cable rails)
www.feeneyinc.com

LifeBreath (energy recovery ventilator)
www.lifebreath.com/us

Miele (appliances)
www.mieleusa.com

NorAire (heat pump/boiler)
https://electromn.com

Resource Furniture (bed/couch in guest room)
https://resourcefurniture.com/product/oslo-215

Revision Solar (solar panels)
www.revisionenergy.com

Sonneman (lighting)
https://sonnemanlight.com

Sun Valley Bronze (lighting)
www.sunvalleybronze.com

## LIPAN ROAD HOUSE

Armony Cucine (kitchen cabinetry)
www.armonycucine.it/en/

Bertazzoni (appliances)
https://us.bertazzoni.com

Caesarstone Quartz (countertops)
www.caesarstoneus.com

Duchateau (prefinished white oak wood flooring)
https://duchateau.com

Duravit (toilets)
www.duravit.us

Emser Tile (porcelain tile)
www.emser.com

Hansgrohe (plumbing fixtures)
www.hansgrohe-usa.com

James Hardie (fiber cement lap siding and smooth panel)
www.jameshardie.com

Mitsubishi (heat pump)
www.mitsubishicomfort.com

Puntotre (bathroom vanities)
www.arredobagnopuntotre.com

Quaker (aluminum windows)
quakerresidentialwindows.com

## LOWRY HOUSE

Fujitsu (air-source heat pump)
www.fujitsugeneral.com

Hearthstone Green Mountain
(wood stove)
www.hearthstonestoves.com

Kohltech (triple-pane
windows)
www.kohltech.com

Life Breath (heat recovery
ventilator)
www.lifebreath.com/us

Plasti-Fab (insulated
foundation)
www.plastifab.com

Rheem (hybrid hot water heat
pump)
www.rheem.com

Vetta (triple-glazed doors in
entry, porch, and house to
garage)
www.vettawindows.com

Whirlpool (heat pump clothes
dryer)
www.whirlpool.com

## MALIBU HOUSE

Alux windows (aluminum
windows)
www.aluxinfissi.eu/en/

Benjamin Moore (paint)
www.benjaminmoore.com

Bosch (appliances)
www.bosch-home.com

Caesarstone (countertop and
backsplash)
www.caesarstoneus.com

Corian (shower walls)
www.corian.com

Daltile (flooring)
www.daltile.com

Duravit (freestanding tub)
www.duravit.us

Eco-Smart Fireplace
https://cdn.ecosmartfire.com

Grohe (faucets)
www.grohe.us

Mohawk (engineered
hardwood flooring)
www.mohawkflooring.com/
wood

RenewAire (energy recovery
ventilator)
www.renewaire.com

Rheem (electric water heater)
www.rheem.com

The Shade Store (sunshades)
www.theshadestore.com

Wayne Dalton (garage door)
www.wayne-dalton.com

## MARIS ADU

Bellmont Cabinets (kitchen
cabinets)
www.bellmontcabinets.com

Baldwin (hardware)
www.baldwinhardware.com

James Hardie (Fiber cement
siding)
www.jameshardie.com

Milgard (windows and doors)
www.milgard.com

## MAYNARD HOUSE

Logic Windows & Doors
(triple-glazed, turn-tilt
windows)
https://logicwd.com

Mitsubishi (air-source heat
pump)
https://www.
mitsubishicomfort.com

Lifebreath (heat recovery
ventilator)
www.lifebreath.com/us

Jotul (gas stove)
www.jotul.com

TruExterior Trim (boral)
https://truexterior.com

## OLIVE PASSIVE HOUSE

Awair (monitoring system)
www.getawair.com

Batimet (windows and doors)
www.batimet.com

Daltile (bathroom tile)
www.daltile.com

Fantini (tap and shower heads)
www.tattahome.com/en/

IKEA (kitchen cabinets)
www.ikea.com

Lapitec (countertops)
www.lapitec.com/en

Mitsubishi (mini-split heat
pump)
www.mitsubishicomfort.com

North Solar Screen (exterior
shades)
https://northsolarscreen.com

Stelpro (post-heater)
www.stelpro.com/en/

Stiebel Eltron (tankless electric
water heater)
www.stiebel-eltron-usa.com

The Cabinet Face (cabinet
fronts)
https://thecabinetface.com

Zaborski Emporium (salvaged
sink)
http://zaborski-emporium.
edan.io

Zehnder Comfoair 350 (energy
recovery ventilator)
www.zehnderamerica.com

## PASSIVE NARROWTIVE

Audio Insider (sunscreens,
roller shades, building controls,
automation)
www.AudioInsider.ca

Banner Carpets Ltd (flooring)
www.bannercarpets.ca

Daltile (tile)
www.daltile.com

Eco Spa Canada (hot tub)
www.EcoSpaCanada.com

Flora (plumbing fixtures)
www.fiora.us

James Hardie (fiber cement
siding)
www.JamesHardie.ca

Kayu (hardwood sidings)
www.Kayu.ca

Kuzco Lighting
www.Kuzcolighting.com

Midland Appliance
(appliances)
www.MidlandAppliance.com

Nudura (insulating concrete
forms)
www.nudura.com

Opti-Myst fireplace
www.woodlanddirect.com

Pac Rim Cab (cabinetry)
www.PacRimCab.com

Riobel (plumbing fixtures)
www.riobel.com

Robinson Co. (lighting)
www.Robinsonco.ca

Sherwin Williams (exterior and
interior paint and stain)
www.Sherwin-Williams.com

Small Planet Supply (heat
pumps)
www.SmallPlanetSupply.com

Vetta Windows
www.VettaWindows.com

Vrec Solar (photovoltaic
panels)
www.Vrec.ca

West Eco Panels (structural
insulated panels)
www.WestEcoPanels.com

Zehnder America (energy
recovery ventilators)
www.ZehnderAmerica.com

## THE PINK HOUSE

James Hardie (fiber cement
siding)
www.jameshardie.com

Jaxx Zipline (upstairs sleeper/
sofa)
www.jaxxbeanbags.com

Jeld-Wen (exterior windows
and doors)
www.jeld-wen.com

Spark (gas fireplace)
https://sparkfires.com

Toto (toilets)
www.totousa.com

## PORTAGE BAY
## FLOATING HOME

Canyon Creek (cabinets)
www.canyoncreek.com

Cembrit (fiber cement siding)
www.cembrit.com

Sierra Pacific (windows and
doors)
www.sierrapacificwindows.
com

## THE RALEIGH SIMPLE
## HOME AND ADU
## COTTAGE

Auson (pine tar finish)
www.auson.se

James Hardie (fiber cement
siding)
www.jameshardie.com

LP SmartSide (board & batten
siding)
https://lpcorp.com

Lunos Canada (energy
recovery ventilator)
https://lunoscanada.com

Mitsubishi (air-to-air heat
pumps)
www.mitsubishicomfort.com

## SPARC HOUSE

Active Energies (solar panels)
https://www.activeenergies.
com

A.O. Smith (electric resistance
water heating tank)
www.hotwater.com

Beko (appliances)
www.beko.com

Mitsubishi (heat pumps)
www.mitsubishicomfort.com

RenewAire (energy recovery
ventilator)
www.renewaire.com

## THIMBLEBERRY HOUSE

Alpine Insulation (blow-in-
blanket system)
www.alpineinsulation.com

Artistic Tile (ceramic tile)
www.artistictile.com

Casa Minimo (custom-made
dining chairs, cocktail table,
and benches)
https://casaminimo.com

Cle Tile (backsplash)
www.cletile.com

Clopay (garage door)
www.clopaydoor.com

CP lighting (floor lamps)
www.cplighting.com

Diresco (quartz countertop)
www.diresco.be/en/

GE (appliances)
www.geappliances.com

Honeywell True Fresh (energy
recovery ventilator)
www.honeywellhome.com

Idea Gallery (Baylake
sculptures)
https://ideagalleryart.com

Island Stone (dog wash
flooring)
https://islandstone.com

LP (engineered wood siding)
https://lpcorp.com

Mannington (vinyl plank
flooring)
www.mannington.com

Scathain (custom furniture)
www.scathain.com

Simpson Doors (interior doors)
www.simpsondoor.com

Sonoma Tilemakers (dog wash
walls)
https://sonomatilemakers.com

Trex (porch decking)
www.trex.com

Wilco Cabinetry
https://wilcocabinets.com

Windsor Windows
www.windsorwindows.com

## TROPICAL PANORAMA

Caribbean ICF Solutions
www.caribbeanICFsolutions.
com

Medallion Cabinetry (cabinets)
www.medallioncabinetry.com

New Aged Concrete Coatings
(flooring)
newagedconcretecoatings.
com

PGT (windows)
www.pgtwindows.com

Plaza Doors (glass doors)
www.plazadoorcompany.com

Window and Door Logistics/
Supplier
www.
seaviewbuildingsolutions.com

## VINEYARD VISTA

Daltile (tile)
www.daltile.com

James Hardie (fiber cement
siding)
www.jameshardie.com

JELD-WEN (windows)
www.jeld-wen.com

Kitchenaid (appliances)
www.kitchenaid.com

Pental Quartz (countertops)
https://pentalquartz.com

Simpson (interior doors)
www.simpsondoor.com

TAS Flooring (laminate
flooring)
www.tasflooring.com

Therma Tru (exterior doors)
www.thermatru.com